TOTAL SURVIVAL

TOTAL SURVIVAL

HOW TO ORGANIZE YOUR LIFE, HOME, VEHICLE, AND FAMILY FOR NATURAL DISASTERS, CIVIL UNREST, FINANCIAL MELTDOWNS, MEDICAL EPIDEMICS, AND POLITICAL UPHEAVAL

James C. Jones

Skyhorse Publishing

Skyhorse Publishing books may be purchased in bulk at special discounts for sales promotion, corporate gifts, fund-raising, or educational purposes. Special editions can also be created to specifications. For details, contact the Special Sales Department, Skyhorse Publishing, 307 West 36th Street, 11th Floor, New York, NY 10018 or info@skyhorsepublishing.com.

Skyhorse® and Skyhorse Publishing® are registered trademarks of Skyhorse Publishing, Inc.®, a Delaware corporation.

Visit our website at www.skyhorsepublishing.com.

10 9 8 7 6 5 4 3 2

Library of Congress Cataloging-in-Publication Data is available on file.

Cover design by Tom Lau

Print ISBN: 978-1-5107-3900-0
Ebook ISBN: 978-1-5107-3902-4

Printed in China

CONTENTS

INTRODUCTION

After fifty years of writing, teaching, and advocating for survival preparedness and self-reliance, I have covered about every survival-related subject there is. Most of my materials exist in short articles, class outlines, PowerPoint programs, and notes. I also have a vast library of references and photos from various survival-training activities. While my most original works are devoted to the psychological and philosophical aspects of survival, I do address the more practical "nuts-and-bolts" aspects as well.

The challenge when preparing this book was to organize all the material in a coherent way. There are hundreds of "survival manuals" in publication, and I did not want to simply create another one. No survival book can cover every conceivable aspect of surviving every conceivable situation, so I decided to focus on subjects that I felt were the most likely needs and that I could create useful and practical chapters to cover.

Ten is a rather arbitrary number, but it helps to organize the material into manageable bites of knowledge. As I developed each chapter, I stretched or bundled material to fit the ten-subject standard. In some cases the same item applied to more than one category. For example, water applies to the water chapter, but it also comes up in home survival and in various survival packs. In such cases, I either referred the reader to the appropriate chapter or added some additional information not previously provided. I tried to cover the ten most important items in each category where possible, but there is no point in listing an item unless I could provide some useful information within a reasonable number of pages. So, this guided my choices. When any of the ten items took me a bit out of my knowledge wheelhouse, I did extensive research and combined multiple sources to provide the most useful information within a reasonable space. Some items within a subject chapter inspired more text or illustrations than others, particularly if the subject was not addressed in other chapters.

Where necessary, I have added lists, tables, and other materials at the end of chapters to further enhance their value. Some subjects required significant illustrations while others are primarily text. I used a combination of photos from my personal library, illustrations from military manuals, and some of my own illustrations where needed. While most of the subject material is covered in other survival manuals, I have added my own perspectives based on my fifty years of experiences and study. As I addressed each topic, my self-imposed "ten" theme forced me to organize materials in new ways and look at alternatives not always considered. In many cases I realized that I had some valuable experiences, tips, illustrations, and techniques to contribute to the subject drawn from classes and programs conducted by Live Free USA. My goal here is to share a variety of practical survival skills, principles, and ideas in an easy-to-read format that will aid the reader in becoming stronger, safer, and more self-reliant.

CHAPTER 1
Ten Principles of Survival

None of the survival precautions, methods, procedures, and techniques that are explained and advocated throughout this book will be of any value if your mental state and psychological condition render you unable to function effectively. Mental survival is the fundamental necessity for physical survival. The principles enumerated below are derived from analysis of true survival accounts. Studies of why some people survived fires, plane crashes, assaults, and other deadly situations while others in the same situations perished confirm that these principles made the difference. I have extracted the lessons from these sources and organized them into the following ten principles.

Although the data and concepts were derived from accounts of acute (rapidly developing) disasters—such as tornadoes, floods earthquakes, and epidemics—I realized that they apply equally well to chronic (slow-developing and persistent) disasters, such as economic decline, shortages, unemployment, climate change, and personal family or health issues. Finally, I came to the realization that these principles were the key to success in everyday life. In truth, all of life is a low-intensity survival challenge, and a survival emergency is just a high-intensity life challenge. People who have survived the worst disasters have usually done so by following these principles, and those who have had successful lives have done the same.

Before we get to the ten principles, we need to discuss the importance of the mental aspects of survival.

MENTAL ADJUSTMENT TO THREATS

It is important to understand the stages that the mind goes through when it encounters an unpleasant or dangerous situation. Again, these apply equally to a sudden-hazard event or a developing bad situation. Once we recognize (at least subconsciously) that something is wrong or going wrong, our mind begins to cope. The ten principles are important in determining how quickly and effectively we move from denial to action. In acute emergencies, we go through the four stages within seconds or minutes or we don't survive. In the cases of slow-developing, chronic disasters, the process is slower and we may not even recognize our mental adaptation, but lingering too long before getting to effective action can still result in serious consequences. Time always runs out!

Denial

Denial is often verbalized in such phrases as, "This can't be happening!" "Oh no!" or "You've got to be kidding!" People commonly rationalize scary events to avoid dealing with them: *A fire alarm must be a false alarm. Shots must be firecrackers. Chest pain must be indigestion. The weather can't get any worse. It won't be that bad; surely things will turn around.* While panicking at every slight sign of trouble is certainly unhealthy, it is far more dangerous to ignore clear signs of potential hazard without further consideration. Remember, we are all the descendants of people who heard the rustling in the bushes and ran like hell. The ones who shrugged and said, "It's probably nothing," didn't have descendants.

Deliberation

"What should I do?" You are in immediate or eventual danger. The sooner you get out of the denial mode, the more time you have for deliberation. Indecisive people generally do not survive threatening situations unless they are just lucky. Depending on luck is a lousy survival plan. The ten principles will be of great value at this stage. Move!

Decision

This stage is greatly facilitated by past experience, training, and available resources. People known as "high dread personalities" who have experienced past calamities or have had a challenging life will usually do better at making hard-and-fast decisions under stress.

Action

No course of action is guaranteed to be the right one in true survival situations. The more you know, the more effective your actions can be. Any survival situation is caused by a change in your otherwise stable and safe situation. Therefore, only by changing your own situation (e.g., location, position, status, activity) can you hope to reestablish a "safe and sound" status.

Once you have moved from denial through deliberation to the decision and action phases of survival reaction, these ten important principles must be applied to guide your actions.

1. ANTICIPATE

Those who assume that things will not change or that nothing can go wrong wind up being victims. Those who do "what-if" analysis on potential hazards and trends are ready to survive. While those who say, "This can't be happening!" are still in denial, the survivor is ready to act or has already acted. Survivors are people who quickly move through the stages of denial and deliberation to decisions and actions.

Accepting the possibility or probability that a bad thing may happen to you is essential. The military calls this process OODA: observe, orient, decide, act. Anticipation based on the presumption that if it can happen it will happen and that if it has happened to others it can happen to you motivates actions to avoid, prevent, and, if necessary, survive a disastrous event. If you have poor health habits, you can anticipate serious illness. If your home is cluttered and poorly maintained, you can anticipate an accident or a fire. If others in your field or area are losing their jobs and homes, you can anticipate losing yours. But anticipating winning the lottery or getting a break is dangerous thinking.

Building personal, financial, and material strength is a winning strategy regardless of future events. It's OK to hope for the best, but it's essential to plan for the worst. In industry and government what-if analysis is used to analyze potential for fires, explosions, spills, and other catastrophic events. In these exercises it is assumed that people will do the wrong things, safety valves and devices will fail, and weather conditions will be the worst for the situation. In other words, Murphy's law will be in full effect throughout the emergency. It is amazing how many potential problems are found and eliminated through this process. Look at your lifestyle, habits, home, community, education, job, finances, associations, and the world's conditions and events in a what-if mode. Most serious accidents and disasters are the result of the confluence of two or more factors at just the wrong place and time.

2. BE AWARE

The military calls this "situation awareness." On a big-picture level, this means being aware of the national economic, political, and environmental situations, and the developments in your communities and at your place of employment. What are the trends? What are the developing hazards, shortages, and threats? On a more immediate level, you must develop the habit of observing and analyzing things around you and ahead of you. No texting, no cell phone use, no daydreaming. "Who are those people coming toward me?" "Do I smell smoke?" Be aware of sounds, shadows, light changes, and odors. Know what's going on around you 360 degrees and up and down. Combat veterans have this habit, as do police officers. You should too. Those who have worked in heavy industry (and survived) have this habit. Most others don't. The great majority of accident and crime victims got blindsided because they were blind to incoming hazards.

Listen to your sixth sense. In slow-developing hazards, we have the luxury of using our conscious, analytical mind to make decisions. When danger strikes quickly, we often must depend on instincts and training to detect the hazards and act automatically. But the deeper, primal feeling from our sixth sense is too often ignored or overridden by what we call reasoning or a desire not to appear overcautious or paranoid. These feelings that something is not right when we get a chill or the hairs on the back of our neck stand up are responses to signs and sensations that we cannot consciously recognize or define, but they are very real. Such sixth-sense premonitions usually arrive ahead of any conscious warnings and should put you on guard and get you ready to respond.

Levels of Awareness

Even the military cannot maintain high alert levels indefinitely. While you should always be aware of your surroundings and alert for changes, you can adopt different alert levels depending on your location and situation. Of course, you need not consciously say, "Alert condition yellow!" You just shift awareness as you go through life.

- **Condition red:** This means that a serious threat is imminent, obvious, and unavoidable. You smell smoke, see a weapon being deployed, sight a tornado funnel, or feel the ground start to move. You immediately look for and get to the most available and effective shelter for the situation, or you act fast to escape from the hazard. You prepare to fight with whatever weapons you have or can reach.
- **Condition orange:** This is when an emergency or disaster seems probable. For example, you hear a tornado warning, conclude that approaching individuals appear aggressive and may be armed, recognize signs that the economy is getting shaky, or hear rumors of an epidemic starting. You're not in trouble, but a crisis is coming fast. You need to mentally prepare and gather your equipment. Maybe you ready your weapons or move closer to escape routes or shelter locations. This is not the time to be far from home, without weapons, or have your family dispersed. The better your preparedness efforts have been, the better your survival chances will be now.
- **Condition yellow**: You are safe and no threats are obvious, but you are alert because your location or situation makes you a bit more vulnerable to various hazards. When you are away from home—in the

outdoors, in crowds, or at stores, banks, gas stations, and similar locations—you need to be extra alert. Anytime you are in a high-crime area or there has been criminal activity in your community, be at condition yellow. People are assaulted on their front porches and in their homes all the time. At times of unsettled weather or national unrest, keep your eyes and ears open and watch your six.

- **Condition green:** Sometimes you just have to relax. If you cannot feel safe in your own home or at your workplace most of the time, you probably need to make some serious life changes. When you are in a safe place with people you trust and there are no immediate external threats to worry about, enjoy! The knowledge that you are mentally and materially prepared to cope with emergencies should provide a great sense of security and comfort.

3. BE WHERE YOU ARE

This sounds obvious, but think about it. When we are talking, reading, texting, or playing a game on our cell phone, or have earbuds in our ears, we are mentally *there*, instead of *here*. We tune out what's going on around us. This is okay in a safe environment, such as at home or in an office, but never in an at-risk situation, such as while walking, driving, or riding public transportation. Such habits are an invitation to crime, accidents, and being surprised by developing dangers.

The other application of this directive is when you are already in a hazardous situation. A survival situation requires your being 100 percent at this time and at this place. Any distractions or thoughts about how nice it would be to not be in this place at this time will only make the situation worse and survival less likely. Mental escapism is not helpful in most cases. Constructive and positive "I can get through this" and "What is my best chance?" thinking is what is needed.

At-risk mental states often take us away from the here and now just when we should be the most focused. Disasters and emergencies can make us angry, fearful, frustrated, and distracted. Prolonged stress often results in extreme fatigue. Being in pain, too cold or too hot, extremely thirsty, or hungry is also associated with disaster situations. All these can result in loss of focus on problem solving and safety just when you can least afford errors and accidents. While you may not be able to fully control your emotional state and environmental conditions, being aware of their dangerous, distracting effects and using care and control are critical.

4. STAY CALM

This is easier said than done. If you have followed the first three principles, your reactions are going to be automatic and appropriate. Once you have escaped the immediate threat (e.g., assault, shots, fire), take some slow, deep breaths. Gather your thoughts and follow the next six principles. Remember your calm (or apparent calm) will help others follow your lead. Understanding how your body and mind will react to stress can be helpful in staying calm. Intense training that creates stress is used by the military to condition soldiers to handle combat, but most civilians are less prepared when sudden disaster strikes. You may freeze, panic, or make illogical decisions. The mind may go blank and forget even basic survival knowledge. When shots are fired, flames are spotted, or other threats are taking place, the body is programmed to react in the following ways:

- Blood chemistry changes to improve coagulation.
- Pain relievers and stimulants are released into the bloodstream.
- Respiration and heart rate increase.
- Tunnel vision may develop, wherein you totally focus on the source of danger and are blind to other things (including dangers) around you.

- Non-vital functions are discontinued. This includes digestion that may result in nausea and vomiting, bowels and bladder evacuation, and dryness of the mouth.
- Blood vessels contract, causing increased blood pressure and sweating.

Studies show that people generally react in predictable ways in disasters:
- They look to see what others will do before acting on their own, even when the danger is obvious.
- They follow instructions and a chain of command if provided. Such instructions given with authority are far more effective than those given politely under stress conditions.
- They play the role in an emergency that they play in life. Leaders lead; followers follow; helpers help; predators and parasites do what they do to others.
- They become unified by threats and danger, which can be a good thing or a bad thing.

Psychologically prepared people survive more often than unprepared ones in a true disaster.

How to Calm Yourself

If you have just a few seconds before you must act, do the following breathing exercise to help reduce your stress and improve your performance.

- Inhale slowly for four seconds.
- Hold that breath in for a full four seconds.
- Exhale slowly for four seconds.
- Wait four seconds before inhaling again.
- Do this one or two times before taking your next action.

This also gives you a few seconds to consider your next actions and broaden your vision.

5. EVALUATE

Think about where the situation is going and what your options are. Evaluate the risks of doing nothing versus taking various actions. Consider your own levels of health, knowledge, and resources. Will you have help, or are you on your own? Prioritize risk versus cost and consequences. I have seen "preppers" who bolted at every doomsday prediction. They would literally take to the hills every year or two, abandoning their homes and jobs while dragging their families off to the wilderness. In a few years they had no money, no job, no family, and nothing left with which to survive. I have also seen lots of people put off basic survival and disaster preparedness actions until it was too late, even when the hazard was obvious.

In an acute instant disaster, you have to use these principles immediately to determine your actions, but for slower-developing or anticipated disasters, you can use the following questions to evaluate risk levels and priorities for preparedness.

- **How likely is this disaster?** Do not be panicked by the big, spectacular Armageddon scenarios. They are possible but much less likely to get you than more ordinary disasters, such as a home fire, tornado, epidemic, or crime. Where you live, where you work, and your lifestyle and economic situation affect your vulnerability most. What kinds of things are happening in your area? What kinds of things are happening to those you know? What has happened in the past?

- **How will it affect me?** Will this event endanger my life? Will it affect me directly or through its effect on the economy, community, or associates? Almost all natural and man-made disasters have some kind of domino or trickle-down effect on everyone.
- **How soon is it likely to happen?** What are the odds of this happening within the next year, five years, or ten years?
- **How prepared am I now?** Do you have what you need? Do you have a plan? Do you know what you need to know? This is called "gap analysis": I am here now, but I need to have this, know this, and plan for this in order to survive.
- **What do I need to do, and how fast do I need to do it?** From the above, you can set goals and establish budgets of funds and time to improve your readiness.

You will probably find five or six issues that you really need to be ready for soon. Some will be basic—e.g., personal health, home safety, storm preparedness—while others may include such larger issues as epidemics, financial collapse, and civil disorders. Remember that little disasters that happen just to you are just as deadly as big events that affect thousands.

6. DO THE NEXT RIGHT THING

Sometimes you can let the enormity of the situation panic you into taking inappropriate actions or giving up. You eat the elephant one bite at a time. Once you know what must be done to survive, focus just on how to take step number one. Don't think too much about the other one thousand steps ahead. In the case of the ongoing shifts in the environment, society, and the economy, the next right thing may well be to shift away from dependency and vulnerability as fast as possible. In the case of an eminent threat (e.g., epidemic, civil unrest, economic collapse), the next right thing is either sustained home independence or effective evacuation of the danger zone to a secure area. The former is usually preferable, but the latter option must be available and well planned. For example, a climber was caught in a blizzard on a mountain. As he tried to get back down, he fell into a deep ice crevasse, breaking an arm and a few ribs. No one knew where he was or would be looking for him, and he would certainly freeze to death within a few hours. He didn't think, *OMG I have to climb fifty feet up the vertical ice wall, then descend down a steep mountain in a blinding blizzard, and then walk miles to help.* No, he just focused on finding a foothold and a ledge to get a few feet up. Then another step and another and another. In this way he rescued himself without ever being beaten by the enormity of his situation.

When I present programs on preparedness, I often encounter people who are suddenly aware of how bad things can get and how unprepared they are. They feel that they will never be able to be prepared soon enough to make a difference. They have defeated themselves before trying. I tell them to go home and put water into some containers, designate a few cans of food for emergency use, and buy some candles. It's not much, but it's a start. Something is always way better than nothing. Once they have taken the first small step toward preparedness and self-reliance, they usually continue and build on that.

7. TAKE CONTROL

In survival, things are happening to you. In preparedness, you are preparing for things to happen to you. This is primarily defensive thinking. In an acute, fast-developing disaster, you have to start happening to the situation using your knowledge and initiative. The whole point of being mentally and physically prepared is to be able to take control and change the situation in your favor. If you find yourself in the forest without knowing how to get back to where you started, you aren't lost. You know where you are.

You are right here in the forest, and you own this situation. You have a plan, you have resources (natural and man-made), you have knowledge, and, most important, you have willpower. You may find your way out, be found, or become the guy who lives in the forest, but you've got this.

This same attitude must apply to developing threats for which you are preparing. By being proactive, you may be able to prevent or avoid the consequences. Pushing your life forward toward better education, financial security, and personal improvement always increases your chances when the worst happens. Building your strength is happening to the future before it happens to you. While there are all sorts of predictions of what will happen to us and how soon it will happen, this is no excuse for digging in and closing off. When I started advocating and teaching survival back in the 1960s, during the Cold War and the riots, I was told not to bother organizing because the end was coming within a few years at best. They certainly had plenty of evidence for that expectation, yet here we are fifty years later. I came a long way and got a lot done by happening to life instead of waiting for it to happen to me. We should own the future, not fear it. That's the difference between being a survivor and a victim.

8. HAVE WHAT YOU NEED

That sounds simple, but it requires careful anticipation and awareness to have the right stuff where and when you need it. For example, having lots of food and firearms is not what you need when you have a house fire. You need good fire extinguishers now! Having a full nuclear-biological-chemical suit and mask at home will not help in the more likely situation of smoke or biological hazards encountered on the streets. It's not what you have, it's what you have with you that counts. Prioritizing and acquiring skills, supplies, and equipment based on personal and realistic expectations—not popular media scenarios—is critical. The objective is to have safe air, effective personal defense, adequate shelter, clean water, sufficient food, and essential medical care when and where you need it. Of course, we can't carry a full survival pack around all day. Other sections of this book consider what you need to have in your pockets to help get through those first few minutes of emergency when you are on the street. This is the first rung of the ladder of survival materials. You should have more emergency supplies in your locker, desk, or vehicle to help get you through a few days, if necessary. If you can reach home, there is your survival pack if you must keep moving or your more complete supplies to shelter in place for an extended period. The specifics of what you need are addressed throughout this book.

9. USE WHAT YOU HAVE

The accumulation of stuff alone will not ensure survival. You have to know how to use it and use it effectively. You will also be faced with situations where you need to improvise and scavenge to create survival devices. Junk and scraps can be made into needed items. Nature provides food, shelter, fuel, and other necessities when we do not have other options. Survival training greatly increases your options and capabilities with and without manufactured equipment. In today's world we have specially made products for every aspect of survival. This makes us complacent and dependent. A good drill is to take every survival item you have and ask yourself, "What if I had to do without this?" and then "What could I use in place of this?" Know how to use each item and know how to do without it—then you are a true survivor.

Another exercise is to look at common household items and ask what else this could be used for or made into in an emergency. Could it be a weapon? Could I make a light out of it? Could it be used as a bandage, splint, or tourniquet? Maybe a water or air filter or a shelter? Nature and man provide enough materials to solve most problems. Note, if you only have one item to start with, it should be a knife. The possession of a knife or a multi-tool greatly expands your capacity to modify, improvise, and manufacture things to meet survival needs. It may take multiple steps of improvisation to achieve a survival solution. Suppose you need a screwdriver to get out of a door. What can I fashion the screwdriver out of? What can I use to bend and grind that object into a screwdriver blade? You modify things you have into things you need. Our ancestors did this every day to survive, but we have lost a bit of this ability.

10. DO WHAT IS NECESSARY

That may sound obvious, but it is often the failure to do what was required that resulted in failure to survive. Civilized living has programmed us to adopt habits, fears, and reactions that may be counter to survival necessity. Will we plunge our hand into an open wound to pinch off an artery? Will we hesitate to pull the trigger on an armed assailant? Will we be too shy to strip off cold wet clothing in front of others to prevent hypothermia? Will we trash or abandon expensive equipment in order to escape? Pride, fear, revulsion, fatigue, pain, and false values are mental states that can result in bad decisions. This is not to say that the values of morality, loyalty, and compassion are to be abandoned. If you have abandoned those you have not truly survived as a human being, but surviving may require us to overcome emotional obstacles and mental blocks to solve problems.

During the siege of Leningrad in 1941–42, the residents chopped up and burned even their most precious antique furniture for fuel. Before long, all the dogs, cats, and even rats disappeared. One wonders how some spoiled, materialistic, and finicky Americans would handle these kinds of decisions.

Aron Ralston, whose hand was trapped by a boulder while he was alone in the wilderness in southern Utah in 2003, applied all the other nine principles and exhausted all other options but eventually did what he had to do: cut off his hand to escape and survive.

In the gravest extreme situations, we are forced to revise our values and inhibitions. Retaining valuables or having preserved your modesty or vanity will be of little use if you're dead. Unnecessary death is just stupidity. True survivors, as well as those who succeed at anything, are flexible and adaptable. They bend instead of break.

11. THE ELEVENTH PRINCIPLE: NEVER GIVE UP

Those are my ten principles, but, of course, I have one more! The eleventh principle is "Never Give Up." Having advocated preparedness and greater personal self-reliance for over forty years, I guess I have got that one down. Remember, survival is not about you. You survive for your mission and for what you do for others. Without the will to survive, all your survival skills and equipment will not save you. You must believe that your survival is important, because your family needs you, your friends need you, and your community needs you. You have a mission to complete in life. So your first step in survival is to give of yourself to others and dedicate yourself to a mission. Having done this, you have the foundation of the survival will. Without this, you are inevitably weak and susceptible. I recommend that you (1) write down a personal mission statement today and (2) work on a family mission statement. You can never succeed if you do not define what it is you are trying to achieve.

Several of the above principles are interpretations of concepts set forth in Laurence Gonzales' book Deep Survival, *published by W. W. Norton Inc., which I highly recommend to all serious survival preppers. Reprinted here with permission.*

CHAPTER 2
Ten Disasters to Prepare For

The word "disaster" is derived from combining "dis" (negative or wrong) with "aster" (planetary or stars). So the ancient meaning was a misalignment of the planets. We generally consider disasters to be any events that have massive negative effects on our lives, property, or freedoms. Although the classification of disaster is most often applied to large-scale events causing massive damage and loss of life, any event that injures you or your family, or damages your personal property or life, is a disaster for *you*. Doomsday is not when the world ends—it's when *your* survival plan fails.

Disasters can be caused by natural, geological, meteorological, and even cosmological events, or by the intentional or unintentional actions of humans. Many disasters are only recognized in the proverbial rearview mirror years after they have happened and only as their catastrophic effects have become evident. More often than not, a single disaster sets in motion events that result in additional small and large disasters in the days, weeks, and even years that follow. Disasters are classified as acute or chronic, meaning fast or slow developing.

Acute disasters happen rapidly with little or no warning. Tornadoes, hurricanes, fires, assaults, explosions, most epidemics, civil disorder, and power outages are examples of acute disasters that are obvious, immediate, and require effective preparedness and fast reaction to survive. *Chronic disasters* are often stealthy, developing slowly and lulling people into putting off countermeasures until it's too late. A declining economic system, rising unemployment, increasing crime and corruption, shifting weather trends, developing shortages, increasing prices, and an emerging health crisis from resistant diseases are examples of what could be classified as chronic disasters. Take that annoying sniffle that turns out to be pneumonia or that distant rumble that eventually brings a killer storm. You can do a lot to lessen the impact of such an event before the worst effects are felt and you must prepare for them to become full-blown catastrophes combined with associated acute disasters as time goes on.

SURVIVING THE FIRST SEVENTY-TWO HOURS OF DISASTER

The great majority of emergencies last three days or less. Even if the disaster is an extended cataclysmic event, surviving the first hours and days will be critical.

The detailed skills and materials needed to prepare for and survive most disasters are covered elsewhere in this book, but each type of emergency has some specific actions and techniques that are necessary to survive. Those will be covered in this chapter.

Before we explore the specific imperatives of each disaster situation, let's consider the physical and psychological priorities common to all disasters in chronological order from the first seconds through the first three days. Keep in mind that the future holds events and trends that may be nationwide in scope and months in length, requiring much greater levels of personal preparedness. But here we will limit our analysis to the first seventy-two hours of any disaster scenario. We will establish a chronological examination of a general, nonspecific disaster and consider the challenges, needs, and actions required to survive at each point in time. Keep in mind that failure at any of the time points makes the remaining time irrelevant, since you're dead.

First Minute

While some disasters occur over hours or days, many others are instantaneous. There may be an explosion, an earthquake, or an assault, or you may wake up to a smoke-filled house. In such cases everything depends on actions in that first minute or two. Your options will depend on your training, planning, and the items that are immediately available to you. Bullets, blast, debris, smoke, heat, flying objects, and flames are in your immediate environment. In some cases, such as fires and civil disorders, you may need to escape to a safer location. But if bullets, debris, or blast materials are flying, you must immediately find shelter.

In a collapsing structure (e.g., during an earthquake), it is generally better to lie down next to some strong object (e.g., car, desk, or cabinet) than under it. If you are under the object and it gets compressed, it could injure you, but it will only compress so far, leaving a gap known as the triangle of life holding up the fallen walls or ceiling. Getting behind or under any heavy and secure object can protect you from flying debris, such as in smaller explosions, distant blasts, and strong winds. If immediate shelter is not available, lie flat and cover your head. Most bullets can penetrate furniture, auto bodies, and interior walls. Seek shelter behind brick walls, trees, large appliances, auto engines, and concrete structures. Many Japanese survived the nuclear blasts at Hiroshima and Nagasaki because they were sheltered behind walls or rocks while people a few yards away were incinerated and blown to pieces.

In a burning building, the air a few feet off the floor may be hundreds of degrees hotter than the air at floor level. One standing inhalation can shrivel your lungs and burn your airway closed. Roll out of bed, get low immediately, and then crawl to safety. Know the escape routes and have an escape plan for every building you are in. Smoke, dust, hazardous vapors, and soot caused by blasts, fires, storms, or biological hazards can stop your breathing or start a reaction that will be fatal in a few hours. Always carry a small folding N95 dust mask in your pocket and have one in your desk, lunchbox, and bedside drawer.

First Five Minutes

Assuming that you did the right things and survived the first minute of the disaster, you now can improve your chances and deal with immediate problems. This is the time period you have to seek better shelter, escape from the danger zone, and treat life-threatening injuries. If you have that seventy-two-hour kit or other needed items, this is the time to grab them. In many situations, if you cannot get out in five minutes, your chances are poor. Five minutes of exposure to contaminated air, radiation, or excessive heat or cold can kill you. If you are bleeding heavily or going into shock, you must stop the bleeding and get help fast. Most likely, if you cannot escape a structure in five minutes, you are trapped. If this were an oncoming disaster (e.g., tornado), you should be in the best available shelter with your survival items in no less than five minutes.

If you survived a bomb blast or shooting incident, get out of the area immediately. Often there is a second bomb or the shooters return. Bullets and blast fragments may have struck supports, wiring, pipes, or tanks, which may cause a secondary hazard.

First Hour

If you have survived the first few minutes and have made the right moves, your chances of survival are greatly improved. In the first hour, you should either move farther away from the danger area or improve your shelter and start to prepare for the next few days. Evaluate your situation, look around, make plans, calm down, and take control. What do you have that can be used? Can you self-rescue (e.g., dig out)? Can you signal for help? Conduct a self-examination for injuries and treat them (e.g., bandage, splint, clean) as best you can. If you have been contaminated with chemicals, biological agents, or fallout, get out of any contaminated garments or clean them as well as possible. Keep that dust mask on!

First Eight Hours

In this time frame you should have gotten to your best available shelter and treated any serious injuries. In cold or rainy weather, shelter and warmth become imperative. If you are exposed to cold for too long, you will be subject to hypothermia (exposure) and could die. Get into shelter and into dry clothing. That dust mask will reduce heat loss through respiration, so keep it on. Put on the warm hat that should be in your survival kit.

Water also becomes a critical need. Hopefully you can find a source of safe, clean water. You can use four to eight drops of bleach per gallon of water or boil for five minutes to purify suspect water. Although you can, theoretically, last three days without water, your physical and mental state will deteriorate after a day or two, so stay hydrated.

First Twenty-Four Hours

Stay warm, dry, and hydrated, and avoid dangerous areas and people. At this point, there are secondary hazards developing. People may be panicking, and criminals may be roaming the streets and looting stores, houses, and vehicles. Fires may rage out of control. Water and sewer systems may fail, and there may be no lights, so avoid being out after the sun goes down if you can. Your best defenses are camouflage and evasion. You need to avoid exposing your position if you have taken shelter. If you are evacuating, you need to avoid such areas as main roads and commercial areas that will attract looters and gangs. Yes, you need to be armed.

First Forty-Eight Hours

If you are still in shelter, trapped, under attack, or on the road after a full day, you have a serious situation on your hands. This is where you really need the stuff in that seventy-two-hour kit. There will be some water, food, and medical items in there. If you depend on prescription medications or eyeglasses, the kit should have those. You will really start to get hungry by now. Theoretically, you can go without food for three weeks, but after twenty-four hours, the need for food starts to affect your judgment and health. If you have no food in your kit or no access to stored food, then you must start foraging, which in urban and wilderness areas is difficult and hazardous. In many cases you will be competing for limited food supplies with other desperate (and likely armed) people. It is far better to have enough food on hand to avoid this necessity. Now you can evaluate your situation and decide if you need to just hang on or take action to improve your chances. Waiting too long can be fatal, but so can taking unnecessary risks. Reevaluate and improve.

First Seventy-Two Hours

If this is a true seventy-two-hour emergency, all you need to do is hang on. Rest, stay warm, conserve energy, drink water, signal for help, and do nothing to expose yourself to further hazards. This is the time for calm consideration, observation, and maybe cautious reconnaissance. Whatever happened may have now generated a breakdown in law and order, or an epidemic may have broken out. There may still be radioactive fallout or other contaminants in the air. Psychologically you are going to return to a safe mode or a "whatever it takes" mode as you prepare for the days and weeks to come.

Beyond Three Days

In most cases you are going to survive if you make it through three days. However, if it turns out to be an extended, wide-area disaster, where help will not be available for weeks and things will not return to normal for months or longer, your chances of survival are poor unless you have planned, prepared, and stocked up for a longer siege.

SURVIVING TEN COMMON DISASTERS

I selected the following ten disasters because they are the most likely to happen to the most people with the most tragic consequences. Some of them are the most commonly accepted as mass disasters while others, such as home fires and home invasion, are more personal. A disaster is something bad that happens to you and your family regardless of how widespread or limited. Doomsday is when you are unprepared and your survival plan (or lack of one) fails. It is important to keep in mind that big disasters of one kind usually trigger other disasters and hazards. So total preparedness is essential.

1. HOME FIRE WHILE AWAKE

A fire in your home is a true disaster for you regardless of whether it is part of a larger disaster in the region or just your home. In a regional or national disaster, the likelihood of a fire is greatly increased, and with fire departments unable to respond, you are the only one who can prevent the total loss of your shelter and critical survival supplies. A fire takes you from a survival-at-home situation to a survival-on-the-streets situation and greatly reduces your long-term chances for survival.

Fire Prevention

In most cases, your home is your best survival shelter. But in a survival situation, you will probably be using candles, oil lanterns, gasoline generators, and other fire-hazard devices. Keep these in safe locations, well away from paper, clothing, fuels, and other combustibles. Fill gas tanks and lanterns outside, well away from structures. Store flammable fuels outside. Be aware of carbon monoxide hazards. Have both smoke and carbon monoxide detectors in working order. Secure at least two full, large ABC-class fire extinguishers and have one on hand whenever handling fuels.

Incipient Fire Extinguishing

Unless you have a fully functional fire pump and hose system, you cannot hope to put out a structural fire, but if you have immediate and effective fire extinguishers you can put out an incipient fire started by candles, cooking equipment, heaters, or even a Molotov cocktail. You can also put out trash fires, brush fires, and windblown embers from other structures. Good dry chemical extinguishers rated for ABC-class fires are available in many sizes. Class "A" fires are paper, wood, cardboard, and so forth. Class "B" fires are burning liquids, such as gasoline, grease, or kerosene. A Class "C" fire is electrical. Your ABC extinguisher is good for all three, but any kind of water spray can be used to extinguish a class "A" fire.

The most important thing about an extinguisher is where it is stored. It must be right there at hand when the fire starts. A few seconds or a minute spent getting it can mean that the fire is beyond control by the time you get back. So you must have one in the kitchen, garage, furnace room, shop, and anywhere else that you have an open flame (e.g., fireplace, stove, candles) or flammable fuels. Locate the extinguisher away from the most likely fire source. For example, place it near the kitchen door or under the sink but not near the stove.

Using Fire Extinguishers

Don't wait for a fire to occur to read the instructions on the extinguishers! Your local fire department may offer training in their use. (See Chapter 3, "Ten Items for the Prepared Home.") Most extinguishers require you to remove a pin from the trigger/handle before you can depress the trigger. Check the instructions when you buy the extinguisher.

When using a pressurized powder extinguisher, you should stand well back from the fire and aim just short of the front edge of the fire to let the powder roll over the flames. Then sweep back and forth going just past each side and farther in with each sweep until past the back of the fire. Don't squirt the fire. Keep sweeping the spray back and forth. Be sure all flames are out before stopping. Then hold ready to stop a reignition. Don't blast the fire close up—this will only blow burning fuel around.

Be careful not to walk into the fuel as you advance on the fire. It is always best to have a second person at your back with another extinguisher ready. Never let the fire get between you and your escape route, and never try to fight a fire once the room is filled with smoke.

When fighting a class "A" fire, soak the fire thoroughly and then use a shovel or other device to turn over the embers and ashes and soak hot spots. Consider that a fire goes up and out and looks for fuel and air. It may follow vents, electrical openings, and other routes to ignite between walls or in other rooms. Search and extinguish it and stay alert for rekindling for up to twenty-four hours. (See Chapter 3, "Ten Items for the Prepared Home.")

2. HOME FIRE WHILE ASLEEP

You are far more likely to die in a home fire than from most anticipated cataclysmic events. This is particularly true if the fire starts while you are sleeping. If you awaken to a smoke-filled room, do not sit up. The air just above you may be heated to several hundred degrees and filled with toxic gases. Roll out of bed and crawl to the nearest exit. If the bedroom door is closed, feel it for heat before opening it. If it's hot to the touch, you may need to open or break a window to escape. If trapped or you have time, call 911, but you have only seconds to get out! A dust mask and a flashlight kept in the bedside drawer may save your life in the dark, smoke-filled house. Once outside, never return to a burning building, as you will probably not get out again.

You should have trained every member of your family in escaping a fire and have established a meeting place outside. To illustrate the need for training and speed, I offer the following photos that I took at a test fire. This was set up as a sofa fire in a normal-sized living room.

Fifteen to twenty seconds after ignition: Smoke detectors go off. If you spotted this fire and have a good fire extinguisher, you might be able to put it out. If not, you have only about sixty seconds to get everyone out.

Sixty to ninety seconds: Heavy smoke and gases obscure visibility down to a few feet above the floor. You must stay low and get out immediately.

Two to three minutes: The heat of the fire begins to ignite other materials. The TV explodes, and hot, combustible gases fill the room.

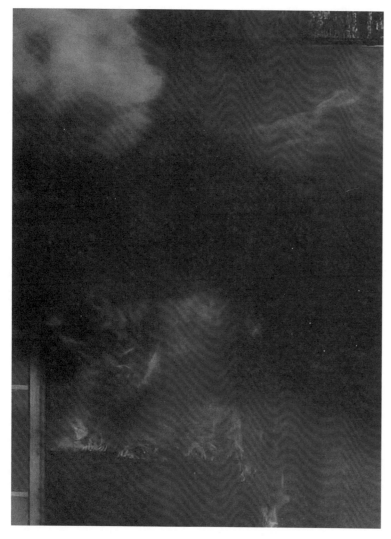

Three to five minutes: A "flashover" of the hot gases explodes the fire throughout the structure.

Five minutes: Fire department arrives on the scene. Even this fire hose would not be enough to extinguish a totally involved structure. The best the firemen can do is prevent the flames from spreading to adjoining structures.

Conclusions

Fire is often an overlooked side effect of other disaster scenarios. Storms, earthquakes, epidemics, economic collapses, and other situations could create ideal conditions for the spread of massive fires through urban and suburban areas. Fire can negate all your survival planning and preparations. Fire prevention, escape, and survival must be part of your survival planning and equipment priorities.

3. HOME-INVASION INTRUDER

Although I lived in one of the highest-crime regions in Chicago, no one ever made the mistake of invading my home. For this section, I did get a lot of information from people who have had this experience. I also had access to urban and suburban crime reports that show what kinds of entries are common.

Intruder Prevention and Survival

- Don't hesitate to call the police at the first sign of attempted entry. An elderly couple I know refused to answer the door when three men were banging on it one Halloween night. Then the same men banged on the rear door until they broke in. The men beat the couple and stole most of their valuables. Obviously, the homeowners should have called the police when the first incident started.
- Do not open your doors to strangers. The would-be intruders may dress as utility workers or claim to be in need of help. Call the utility to confirm any utility workers present. Call the police even if they leave, because they are probably headed for your neighbor's house.
- Never let strangers into your home or let them lure you outside. A major scam is to tell you that you have roof, siding, or drainage damage outside. They lead you out to show you something while an accomplice enters and ransacks your belongings.
- Always lock your doors, even if going a short distance. Unlocked doors facilitate lots of burglaries.
- Attached garages are a prime access point for burglars and home invaders. Residents tend to regard the door from the garage to the home as an interior door, but the garage vehicle door is often open or is far less secure. Have the same deadbolt locks on the garage-access door. Keep the vehicle door closed when not entering or exiting the garage and always lock the garage-to-house door.

- Potential home invaders and burglars may watch your home to see when you are out and when you come in, or they may follow you from work or a place you frequent often. Varying your schedule and routes can help. Be alert for anyone casing your home or following you.
- House entries are often crimes of opportunity. Some people just go around knocking on doors and trying handles. If no one answers, they try other doors. If no one seems to be home, they break in. If the door isn't locked, they just enter. This may be a burglary, but if it turns out that someone *is* home or comes home, you have a possible hostage or murder situation. Lock the doors. Call police if suspicious people are checking windows and doors. Never enter your home if you suspect it has been broken into. If you enter and see evidence of an intruder, get out immediately and call 911. Do not go in looking for the intruder!
- Look around when entering your home. An intruder can slip in behind you as you are driving into your garage or sneak up behind you as you unlock your front door. This is often how a home invasion starts.
- If taken hostage on the street, avoid letting the abductors take you to your home, as this is where they plan to harm or kill you. (See Chapter 6, "Ten Ways to Avoid and Survive Street Crime.")
- There is no doubt that the first thing the intruders will do is take your cell phone and disconnect the landline. A few extra cell phones hidden about may come in handy. Remember, even out-of-service cell phones can be used to call 911.
- Have a code word or phrase worked out with your family to let them know you are being held hostage. The invaders may want you to call a family member or answer a call. This would be a chance to get help without tipping off the intruders.
- If you don't have small children, you may want to consider hiding a few firearms where you can get to them quickly. In addition to the bedside drawer (see Chapter 3, "Ten Items for the Prepared Home"), the living room and kitchen are good places to hide weapons.
- Once you are under the control of the intruders and probably tied up or at gunpoint, your options are greatly reduced. In many cases, intruders will injure or kill victims. If multiple family members are present, running in all directions or breaking through windows to escape is better than waiting for execution. If possible, do this before you get tied up.
- If you do find yourself in this situation, remember that this is your territory. You have some advantages in knowing where things are and places to hide or escape. Think various scenarios through ahead of time.
- Home security systems are great, but if the intruders know about them they can disable them or make you disarm them. Having firearms at home can save your life, but advertising that fact gives away much of the advantage and may even invite burglars when you are not home.

What if the Intruder Enters While You are Asleep?

You awaken to the sound of someone breaking into your home or moving around inside. Hopefully, you have heeded the recommendations in this book and have a phone and weapon in your bedside drawer. You must act quickly before the intruder gets to you and before he realizes you are awake.

- If you can do so quietly, close and lock your bedroom door. This will buy you a bit of time and make it harder for him to hear you calling the police.
- Immediately dial 911. Tell the dispatcher (1) that one or more intruders are in your home, (2) where you and other family members are located, and (3) that you are armed. Stay on the line and follow instructions.

- Do not go looking for the intruder. Take up a defensive position that blocks access to you and your family and offers concealment. Wait for the police.
- If the intruder approaches, you are not obligated to give him a warning (e.g., "Stop or I will shoot!"), but you want to be sure it is actually an intruder and not a family member or the police. Ideally, the preferred outcome is a retreating intruder caught by police, not violence in your home.
- If the intruder ignores the warning and continues toward you and your family, you are clearly justified in shooting. Be sure you are positioned so that the shots will not endanger other family members in adjoining rooms.
- Once the police arrive, put down your firearm and turn on interior lights. You don't want to have the police confuse you with the criminal.
- Regardless of the circumstances of a shooting, you must obey all police instructions and not say anything until you have a lawyer present. Never comment to the press about any self-defense action.

4. CIVIL DISORDER

I lived through the Chicago riots of the 1960s. I was just a few blocks from the looting and burning buildings, and I knew many people who lived in those areas. Rioting and looting are usually limited to high-population commercial districts, government facilities, and areas nearby. Areas that are strictly residential or industrial are usually not targeted. If you live in one of the riot-prone areas, your chances of survival are bleak. Your only option is to get out ahead of the event because your chances of stopping a mob of lawless insurgents and the fires they will start are slim to none. Of course, your best bet is to not reside in such areas to begin with. But if this is unavoidable, you should have plans and routes of escape and to get home that avoid heavily populated, densely built commercial and government areas. Public transportation and major expressways are also targets for violence (e.g., shooting, robbery) and should be avoided. Outside the violence and chaos of the riot zones, there are three effects that spread into adjoining communities: crime and gangs, fires, and loss of services.

Crime and Gangs

Since the police are completely occupied or disabled, individual criminals and gangs will take the opportunity to commit acts they may not have contemplated in normal times. Carjacking, rape, robberies, and assaults and killings will increase. Stay off the streets! Burglaries, home invasions, and arson will increase as well. Stay home and be ready to respond. (See Chapter 3, "Ten Items for the Prepared Home.") The ability to stay home and defend your abode for extended periods is the most important survival capacity of all.

Fires

Uncontrolled fires from looted and torched stores and business may spread to adjoining residential areas. Even small fires in homes that would normally be controlled by the fire department can engulf whole communities when this service is unavailable, especially in closely packed neighborhoods and apartment complexes. Obviously, you need to be able to put out your own fires (see Chapter 3, "Ten Items for the Prepared Home") and extinguish embers, but you must consider evacuation well in advance of a spreading conflagration. Mass fires and even firestorms can sweep away whole communities in minutes. Get out of the downwind path and seek lakes, rivers, and open areas clear of flammable and combustible materials.

Loss of Services

During the riots in the 1960s, we were safe at home but could not safely get to our jobs, grocery stores, or other necessities. People who became ill or were injured could not get an ambulance or reach a hospital. In some cases, the fires knocked out power lines. Of course, there were no police or fire services for normal crimes or home fires. This situation lasted for about ten days but could be longer in the future. As stated before, you should be prepared to hold out at home for extended times but also be able to run if necessary.

5. EPIDEMICS AND PANDEMICS

For the purposes of this discussion, I include viruses and bacterial forms of infectious disease. Most epidemiologists and the Center for Disease Control (CDC) state that it is just a matter of *when,* not *if,* a massive, worldwide epidemic occurs. Based on the actions of government agencies in planning and stockpiling medications, this is the agency's worst fear. The combination of population densities and world travel guarantee that any virulent and potent biological agent will spread and be out of control before it is even detected.

Plagues in medieval Europe and Asia killed one-third to two-thirds of the populations before the thinned population and surviving immune systems burned them out. Modern medications and sanitation systems have reduced the occurrences and severity of plagues for the past few centuries, but these very defenses have created the probability of truly widespread and disastrous epidemics in our time. The combination of an overpopulated world located mainly in over-concentrated cities and decades of being overprotected with disinfectants and overmedicated with antibiotics has turned today's populations into a growth medium in a petri dish. Our weakened immune systems mean that any new virus will find a target-rich environment.

Modern mass transportation means that every one of us comes into contact with the biological residue left by hundreds and thousands of people. Potential illness and death fly from Europe and Africa, take buses and trains, ride elevators, and linger on shopping carts, door handles, and products for sale. Of course, most of these biological agents are harmless or cause only minor illnesses, but sooner or later (probably sooner) one of them will not be so innocuous. Millions of unknown viruses and mutations that have not been recognized, much less prepared for, could take root. Medical laboratories are continuing to experiment with various biological agents in their efforts to cure or treat existing diseases. Many of these altered viruses would find the human body with no defenses if accidently released. Smallpox (*Variola major*) was declared eradicated in 1980 and inoculations ended, but there are small stocks of the virus kept by the Russians and the United States for research purposes. There may still be other hidden reserves as well.

We now have a population with no immunities to these eradicated viruses. An accidental release of such material or the deliberate spread of them by some unstable laboratory employee could end life as we know it—or even life period. And, of course, there are the rogue nations and terrorists who already have a variety of potent biological agents available. Tuberculosis is still common in Third World nations and is highly contagious. Massive refugee populations are now flowing from underdeveloped places to Europe and America. Many of these people may be carriers. When you consider the above realities, it is truly a miracle the biological "big one" has not struck already. Being involved in the emergency medical systems and community response planning for urban areas, I can tell you that the plans probably won't work, and the professionals know it.

Impact and Effect

The obvious impact of a widespread epidemic would be the disablement and deaths of millions or hundreds of millions of people. Even if we assume a best case epidemic of, say, 10 to 20 percent fatalities and 50 to

60 percent disabilities of two to six weeks, the civilization still collapses and millions more die as a result of violence, starvation, exposure to cold and heat, and other diseases. Because of our highly dependent and technologically sensitive world, the lack of people to sustain critical systems would quickly demolish order and safety. There would be no one to respond to fires or police calls; no one to keep sanitation pumps, water pumps, and electrical systems running; no one to deliver food, medications, and fuel; no one to keep the virtual money in the banking and financial systems from evaporating. They will all be sick, dead, or at home protecting their own families.

The resulting desperation and shortages will have the cities in flames and the streets like war zones within weeks. The effects of failed water systems and sanitation (i.e., human waste and garbage) will initiate such diseases as cholera, typhus, malaria, and a host of other viral and bacterial infections. As with many other disaster scenarios, your best defense is a well-stocked home, where you can ride out the epidemic without exposure. This is the most extreme situation with a total breakdown of the grid and law and order. The more urban the area, the worse the effects. After the first week or so, the worst of the looting, panic, and disorder will pass as people will have either died, recovered, evacuated, or remain entrenched at home.

Good hygiene and early isolation are the most effective defenses against a general epidemic. Washing hands frequently, using hand sanitizers, and avoiding touching the face are habits that can protect you before any sign of an epidemic appears. You should have a good supply of N95 respirators, bleach, examination gloves and Tyvek suits, splash goggles, antibiotic soap, and heavy-duty plastic bags.

Here are some important actions to help survive an epidemic.

- Be alert for signs of an impending epidemic: radio, TV, or Internet chatter; hospital emergency rooms suddenly overloaded with similar symptoms; and a sudden drop in work or school attendance. It's a good idea to know folks at local hospitals and EMS facilities because they will be the first ones to notice changes and also to get notifications.
- At the first hint that an epidemic may be on the way, increase your personal hygiene habits of washing your hands after handling such publicly used items as door handles and shopping carts. Avoid crowded venues, such as restaurants, theaters, stores, and public transportation facilities when possible. Do not be shy about carrying and wearing an N95 dust/mist respirator if necessary. Avoid hospitals and medical facilities unless absolutely necessary.
- When to stop going to school or work is an individual decision. Most employers are going to wait too long before shutting down and will probably not be paying for time off until people are actually sick, by which time others will have been exposed. If you have vacation time, use it right away.
- You should already have enough food, water, and other supplies for an extended period of home isolation. If you can add more supplies before panic sets in, do so. But don't risk injury and exposure once an epidemic is in full effect. Stay home until the period of communicability has fully passed.
- If you can get to your community's medication and immunization centers without undue exposure to people or other hazards, do so. Countywide systems are in place in most areas to distribute stocked medications, but there may or may not be an effective treatment available for the pathogen involved, and there may not be enough healthy volunteers to do the transportation and distribution.
- If members of your family have been out and potentially exposed, they should be decontaminated and isolated until it is clear that they are not infected. All contaminated clothing should be abandoned outside or in a sealed entranceway. The individuals should be washed down with an antibiotic soap and water or a 10 percent bleach solution and rinsed before entering the home and dressing. They should then be quarantined in a separate room and everyone coming in contact with them must wear a mask (N95) until the period of incubation has passed. Everything they touch or use (e.g., utensils, bathroom, bedding) will need to be handled with gloves and mask and sanitized after use.

- If you or a family member exhibits signs of infection, you have two choices. If the medical facilities are still functioning, and can be reached safely, and are offering effective treatments, get there immediately. If going to a medical facility is not an option, you will need to provide the best care you can at home while trying to avoid contamination. Unfortunately, if you are isolated with an infected person, your chances of avoiding the disease are slim. Most communicable diseases are marked by fever, lethargy, sweating, vomiting, incontinence, and, in some cases, internal bleeding. Managing the fever and maintaining hydration are essential to any hope of recovery. (See dehydration under "Ten Medical Skills You Should Know" chapter.)

On the following page are the basic instructions for fitting an N95 respirator. Getting a good fit is very important in order to achieve real protection.

Homemade Mask for Biological Agents

Mix one tablespoon of bicarbonate of soda with one cup of water. Mix the solution well and soak a cloth or handkerchief in it. Wring out till damp and secure over nose and mouth.

If you are decontaminating an exposed person or treating an exposed or infected person, wearing a gown along with gloves and mask is a good idea. The suit can be peeled off, avoiding contact with the skin and clothing, or decontaminated prior to removal. The mask and gloves should come off last.

Decontamination

Now that we have kept the bad stuff off our skin and out of our lungs, we need to remove the contaminants and contaminated coverings without transferring them back into and onto our bodies. This process is called decontamination. Of course, we want to do this when we are outside the danger zone or at the entrance to more effective shelter (e.g., underground for fallout, enclosed from biological or chemical) locations. Ideally, this is a two-person job, with both individuals wearing protective clothing. It should be done in a location that will not permit contaminated runoff, spray mists, or dusts to contaminate other safe areas.

There are three steps to effective decontamination:

1. Gross decontamination involves simply brushing off or rinsing off any surface contaminants, as well as dumping any contaminated gear that will not be needed.
2. Thorough decontamination is accomplished by the use of pressurized water (not high pressure) with a neutralizing or disinfecting solution. A 10 percent bleach-water solution is best for biological contaminants. Soap and water will clear most chemical and fallout materials. Plain water used copiously will be less effective but may be adequate. The best device for spraying is a commercial pump garden sprayer. Keep a clean one handy at home. They are also good for fighting small class "A" fires and general hygiene tasks.

PROPER MASK-FITTING STEPS

What is often referred to as a fit test* is actually a seal check. Seal fit and check steps are as follows:

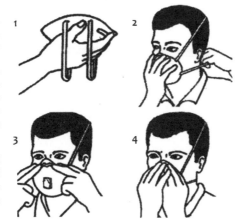 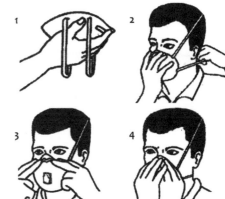

1. Cup the respirator in your hand and place on your face with the bands behind the head, as shown in Fig. 1.

2. Adjust the band above the ears and then the one on the neck to a tight fit (Figure 2).

3. Use your fingertips to form the nosepiece to fit the bridge of the nose (Figure 3).

4. Place both hands over the entire respirator and inhale sharply (Figure 4). Negative pressure should be felt inside the respirator. If air leaks in around the nose or sides adjust the nosepiece and/or straps and try again. Do not enter a contaminated area until you are sure that you have a good seal.

Fit testing is a required OSHA test involving smoke or scents and is performed by technicians.

Tyvek suit for decontamination. Credit: Wikipedia/Jarek Tuszyñski/ CC-BY-SA-3.0.

1

With both hands gloved, grasp the outside of one glove at the top of your wrist, being careful not to touch your bare skin.

2

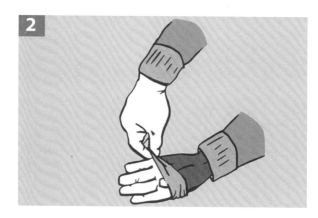

Peel off this first glove, peeling away from your body and from wrist to fingertips, turning the glove inside out.

3

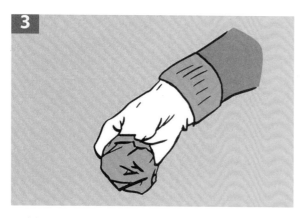

Hold the glove you just removed in your gloved hand.

4

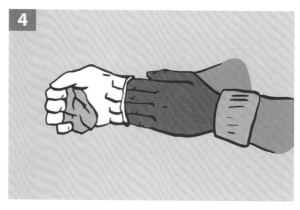

With your ungloved hand, peel off the second glove by inserting your fingers inside the glove at the top of your wrist.

5

Turn the second glove inside out while tilting it away from your body, leaving the first glove inside the second.

6

Dispose of the gloves safely. Do not reuse the gloves.

Degloving Procedure: Clean your hands immediately after removing gloves and before touching any objects or surfaces. At no time does the hand contact the outside of the glove. Thorough hand-washing should still follow degloving to ensure safety. Always bag contaminated gloves, masks, and clothing as they are removed. Credit: Workers' Compensation Board of British Columbia.

Proper Mask-Fitting Steps

3. Peel off the protective clothing, minimizing any contact with the clean clothing and skin underneath. Step out of the foot covers onto an uncontaminated surface. Remove the face mask and then peel off the gloves.

Below are just a few of the potential epidemic diseases that might appear in a survival situation. It is important to know the incubation time for each to understand how long to maintain isolation and expect symptoms to appear. The duration can help determine when it may be safe to come out of isolation. Even epidemics with a low mortality rate could result in serious disruptions of public services, supplies, and the economy, leading to further disasters.

DISEASE	INCUBATION PERIOD AFTER EXPOSURE	EFFECTS	MORTALITY RATE	PERIOD OF INCAPACITA-TION
Anthrax (respiratory)	2 to 3 days	Flu symptoms: chest discomfort, shortness of breath, coughing, high fever, brain inflammation	95 to 100 percent *	4 to 5 weeks
Bubonic plague	2 to 6 days	Nausea, vomiting, fever, headache, bloody diarrhea, enlarged lymph nodes, coma	95 to 100 percent	1 to 5 weeks
Typhoid fever	7 to 12 days	High fever, rash, weakness, headache, diarrhea, sore throat	10 percent	14 to 60 days
Typhus	6 to 15 days	Severe headache, fever, chills, enlarged lymph nodes, muscle and joint pain, rash, mental stupor	10 to 40 percent	15 to 60 days

(continued)

DISEASE	INCUBATION PERIOD AFTER EXPOSURE	EFFECTS	MORTALITY RATE	PERIOD OF INCAPACITATION
Encephalitis	5 to 15 days	Flu-like symptoms, confusion, headache, balance problems, seizures, coma	1 to 80 percent	7 to 60 days
Q fever	15 to 18 days	High fever, muscle and joint pain, headache, cough, chills, nausea, diarrhea, vomiting	0 to 15 percent	7 to 15 days
Yellow fever	3 to 6 days	Headache, fever, muscle and joint pain, vomiting, diarrhea, red eye, jaundice	40 to 80 percent	7 to 14 days
Smallpox	7 to 17 days	High fever, fatigue, nausea, vomiting, diarrhea, widespread blister-like rash	30 to 35 percent **	15 to 30 days
Ebola	5 to 10 days	Sudden-onset fever, fatigue, headache, vomiting, diarrhea, rash, internal and external bleeding	90 percent	15 to 25 days
Tularemia (pneumonic)	7 to 60 days	Dry cough, chest pain, breathing difficulty, fever, diarrhea, nausea, vomiting	30 to 40 percent	50 to 90 days

* In pneumonic form
** Permanent blindness is a common aftereffect of smallpox, particularly in children.

6. EARTHQUAKES

I live in the Great Lakes area, where only very small quakes occur, but on one trip to California I experienced a 6.1 magnitude quake (what are the odds?) and later was involved in the repair and emergency planning for an industrial site after the big San Francisco quake of 1989. When the very earth begins to move and buildings and highways sway, there is no escape, but you can do a few things to improve your chances.

- If in bed when the shaking starts, roll out of bed and lie flat, face down. It is almost impossible to walk or run during a serious quake. Once the shaking stops, you can get out of the building.
- Do not take elevators after an earthquake, as the shafts may be damaged or the power may fail.
- If you are outside, get clear of tall buildings. Facades may fall off or windows may break, showering debris and glass below.
- As soon as you can, turn off your gas and electrical supply, as there may be gas leakage or short circuits that could cause an explosion or fire. Inspect your home for structural damage or hazards, such as damaged stairways, leaking water, and jammed doors.

- Getting under a bed, desk, or other furniture is not advisable for earthquakes, where the main hazard is collapsing structures. If the building collapses, the furniture, and you, will be crushed. Not even a car can stand up to this force; those caught on the Bay Bridge in 1989 were crushed under the heavy debris. The safest location is right at the base of a wall or next to your car, desk, or similar strong object. Yes, these will be crushed but not flattened completely. Even heavy debris will stop and be held up a few feet on either side of the crushed object, leaving a gap. This is known as the "triangle of life," where most survivors are found. (See Chapter 12, "Ten Shelters You Should Know How to Build.")

7. TORNADOES AND HURRICANES

Tornadoes

Living in the Midwest, I have had a variety of experiences with tornadoes. Fortunately, I have not experienced any direct hits, but I have seen the funnels and the damage close up. Tornadoes can develop out of thunderstorms, striking quickly and powerfully. They can completely destroy a brick structure and throw vehicles and even railroad cars hundreds of yards. Their chief danger is from flying debris that can move with such force that it penetrates solid walls. Victims can also be thrown through the air or buried under falling debris. There is usually little warning and little or no time to react. You must anticipate and be ready.

- Be aware of weather trends. Listen to the radio or have an emergency alert radio or app on your phone.
- Take early precautions and preparations for sheltering, evacuating, and dealing with flooding as needed.
- You should have preselected a shelter area in your home. The best spot is in the center of the basement under a sturdy table or workbench. If there is no basement, a center room, hallway, or bathroom (lie in the tub covered with a thick blanket) may be best. (See Chapter 12, "Ten Shelters You Should Know How to Build.")
- Remember, tornadoes move very fast! Don't hesitate and don't stop to gather up items. You should have what you need in your shelter already.
- Tornadoes can hide in rain or be invisible at night, so if the weatherman says it's coming—take cover!
- As soon as you can, turn off your gas and electrical supply, as there may be gas leakage or short circuits that can cause an explosion or fire. Inspect your home for structural damage.

Tornadoes are no longer confined to the Midwest and Great Plains areas. They can strike anywhere with little warning, and they have devastating power. The Fujita scale, which measures tornado intensity, should indicate just how important it is to have a plan and a shelter.

The Fujita Scale

RATING	WIND SPEEDS	DAMAGE
F-1	73 to 112 mph	Shingles ripped off roofs, mobile homes flipped
F-2	113 to 157 mph	Boxcars turned over, siding ripped off buildings, cars overturned, windows broken, trees uprooted
F-3	158 to 206 mph	Exterior walls and roofs blown off, metal building collapsed, forests and farms severely damaged
F-4	207 to 260 mph	Few walls left standing, concrete blocks and heavy debris thrown great distances
F-5	261 to 318 mph	Homes destroyed and debris blown away, schools and other large buildings heavily damaged, roofs and walls removed and top floors demolished

Turning off the Electricity and Gas Supplies

Tornadoes (as well as floods, earthquakes, and hurricanes) often damage electrical lines and gas lines inside the building. This can result in fires and explosions that can cause further injuries and complete destruction of the structure and its contents. Electrical power and gas should be shut off if your house is damaged or if you need to evacuate in anticipation of a disaster.

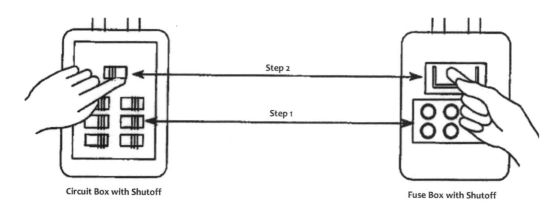

Proper method for turning off the electricity. First shut off individual breakers or pull individual fuses and then shut off the main breaker or pull the main fuse.

Gas Meter and Shutoff Valve

Gas Meter and Shutoff Valve

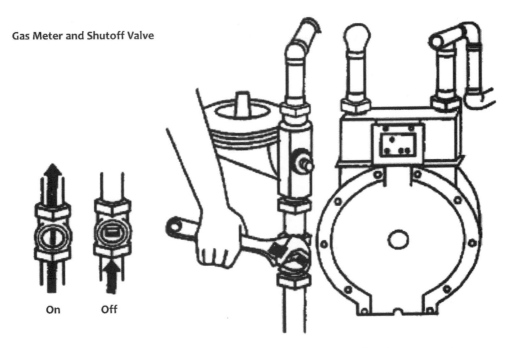

On   Off

Proper way to turn off the gas supply. Once this is done, you should contact the gas company to have it turn the gas back on safely.

Hurricanes

Hurricanes, which most of us generally associate with coastal areas, can bring their winds and torrential rains much farther inland. In fact, it was the confluence of two leftover hurricanes in 2008 that brought flooding to my northern Indiana region. Indiana now has a hurricane emergency plan.

Hurricanes are usually predictable up to a few days in advance, but their specific effects on an area are not easily predicted. While the winds are usually less strong than with tornadoes, they are prolonged and come with long periods of torrential rains that may last several days. The chief hazards are flying debris and flooding.

- Those living in hurricane-prone regions should always have available plywood for boarding up windows.
- You should have a family hurricane plan and an established rendezvous point out of the danger zone if you get separated.
- Unlike with tornadoes, there is usually time to prepare for or evacuate ahead of a hurricane's arrival.
- Anytime a hurricane is likely for your area, keep the gas tanks for all your vehicles full at all times.
- If anticipating a hurricane, bring in or secure all loose outdoor items (e.g., lawn chairs, tables, umbrellas) that can become flying debris.
- Turn freezers and refrigerators to the coldest setting to prolong food life through any power interruptions.
- You should always have a week's supply of water and food in the home, as well as a first aid kit, rescue tools, and emergency lighting. (See Chapter 3, "Ten Items for the Prepared Home.")
- Those living near the coast or in flood-prone areas should seriously consider evacuation. Take the precautions listed below for flood survival.

- Always turn off the gas and electricity before evacuating.
- While government agencies will try to manage evacuation routes and shelters, their efforts may be inadequate. You may be stuck on the highway as the hurricane hits, unable to reach a shelter or safe area, or you may be forced to continue on foot through hurricane conditions. For all these reasons, you must have with you your own evacuation pack or full survival pack.

If you are sheltering in place during a hurricane, stay inside in center rooms, away from windows. Hurricanes that pass directly over you will have an eye that is relatively calm before the second side hits. Don't be fooled into thinking the worst has passed and go outside.

8. FLOODS

If you live anywhere near a river, seacoast, or low-lying flood plain, you have some potential for flooding. Even if the area has never flooded before, that does not mean it will not do so in the future. If it has flooded before, then it most likely will again. I moved into a relatively safe area and experienced the so-called two-hundred-year flood of the region just four years later. I learned a lot about flood response that year. When the National Guard is unloading boats on your front lawn, it cannot be a good thing!

- Don't get complacent. Residents in lower areas who had seen minor flooding before advised me that I was overreacting when I recommended that they evacuate. "Oh, it never gets this far," they assured me. The fire department evacuated them by boat later in the day. Assume that the water *can* reach your home.
- Keep all your emergency supplies and other valuables in waterproof tote bins, and not in cardboard boxes and plastic bags. This will facilitate rapid movement from flooding basements and easy loading for evacuation. I had all my stuff upstairs in about an hour before the water got close. I had the most essential stuff in my truck soon after.
- Just because the river has crested does not mean it will not continue to rise in some areas. Retention pond releases and winds can raise the level and reach homes not affected by the original flooding.
- Do not keep important records or valuables in the basement but, if you must store them there, move them immediately if flooding is likely. Lots of folks lost all their financial, legal, and family records during the flood in my area.
- Have a generator to run your sump pump and have a backup pump to keep the basement dry. Flooding is often accompanied by power outages.
- Rubber boats can come in handy for escape and to remove items from a flooded home. If you live in a flood-prone region, such a craft should be considered a basic survival item.
- Any amount of flooding in a home will cause significant damage. I was a volunteer for cleaning up some of this damage during our flood. Virtually everything had to be torn out: carpeting, furniture, appliances, furnaces, water heaters, interior walls and doors, and even wiring and plumbing in some cases. We used garden sprayers with a 10 percent bleach-to-water solution to decontaminate and demold everything that remained. Then lots of fans and time to dry everything out before replacement could begin.
- Be aware that even if your home is not completely flooded, the pressure on the exterior walls of the foundation can do significant damage and even render your home a total loss.
- Opportunists descend as soon as the waters recede. Get valuables out of your abandoned home and into a locked storage facility as soon as possible. Do not sign anything or authorize any repair work without consulting your insurance company.
- Never go into a basement where the electrical outlets or electrical appliances (e.g., freezer, furnace) are underwater. You can be electrocuted doing this.

Keep a wrench close to your gas meter. *Caution*: After you turn the gas off, you should have the gas company turn it back on.

All that's left of a house that blew up because the gas was left on when the owner evacuated. The gas dryer floated up and severed its gas line, filling the house with gas. The security light timer turned on the lights at exactly 7:00 p.m. and BOOM! The explosion also totaled three other homes.

Below: Many residents experienced damage just because they didn't have a pump or didn't move items to a higher room soon enough.

- If flooding is anticipated, evacuate children and the elderly in advance. They are in more danger during evacuation from an already-flooded area.
- When evacuating your home, be sure to turn off the power at the main breaker if it is not in a flooded basement. Turn off the gas at the main valve as well.

During this flood, firemen used rubber boats for rescues, and residents used boats as well.

9. LOSS OF UTILITIES AND SERVICES

The consequences of losing utilities and municipal services are covered extensively throughout this book. We all depend on what is generically referred to as "the grid" to light our homes, keep us warm, remove wastes, make food available, protect us from crime, put out fires, and care for us if we are injured or ill. Almost every form of disaster offers the potential for short-term, long-term, or even indefinite loss of these services. An epidemic could leave the water pumps, generator stations, and sanitation facilities unmanned. An electromagnetic pulse (EMP) or a cyberattack could destroy vital infrastructure and transportation system. Any one or a combination of such occurrences can have catastrophic effects on what has become a "fridge civilization."

In the absence of water and electricity, high-density, urban areas would descend into chaos within days. A week's interruption of these vital services could destroy the economy and result in millions of deaths and billions of dollars in destruction. Rural areas would need to revert to nineteenth-century living while suburban areas would need to adapt and work together to recover. Responsible citizens should always be ready to get through a few weeks of regional interruption of utilities and services. The best option is to develop alternative sources and seek a more sustainable living system. You don't have to get off the grid, but you shouldn't be dependent on it either. (See Chapter 3, "Ten Items for the Prepared Home.")

10. EVACUATION

Floods, forest fires, hurricanes, and other disasters often call for mandatory evacuations. I have discussed the decisions and challenges of evacuation in other parts of this book. In mandatory evacuations, routes and destinations are usually dictated by government agencies and enforced by military personnel. Where you go and what you take with you are controlled. Recent mass evacuations have been ineffective and dangerous for evacuees even for localized and temporary emergencies. Attempted mass evacuations (spontaneous or ordered) for truly large-scale or long-term disasters would probably result in chaos and panic. The would-be survivor would be well advised to make alternative and independent plans.

For most of my life, I lived in high-crime, low-income areas adjoining heavy industry and commercial development well into the center of the urban environment. The challenges of survival and escape from such locations are numerous and daunting. During these decades I had to maintain both shelter-in-place and evacuation capabilities for myself and others. I participated in numerous test evacuations with groups and families. Later in life, I became a safety manager for a large industrial facility. In that capacity I was responsible for developing practical evacuation plans for several hundred employees in a number of disaster scenarios. Finally, as a lifetime survivalist, I have studied the experiences of those who have actually faced the necessity of escaping from European and Asian cities during wartime bombings, invasions, and persecutions.

From the 1960s through the 1980s, the primary evacuation scenario was based on nuclear war. Your option was to evacuate every time there was tension between the United States and the Soviet Union (which was often) or wait until the sirens went off, at which time it was probably too late. Today's urban evacuation scenarios are more varied and complicated. Worsening civil disorder, spreading epidemics, and lack of water and food supplies may force you to evacuate after a period of days. Floods, uncontrolled fires, gang assaults, or nuclear/biological/chemical contamination may necessitate immediate flight with minimum preparation. The following considerations are based on my many years of planning, replanning, and testing urban escape routes.

Considerations: Time and Distance

The farther into the urban area you live, the harder it is to escape. The gauntlet of blocked streets, bridges, and overpasses; shooters; civil disorder; fires; and other hazards multiplies with every mile between you and open country. Areas on the fringes of the city or into the true suburbs are far easier to escape from or even hold out in. Consider this when relocating, even though jobs and family obligations may dictate where you live.

The sooner you move to evacuate, the better. Once even a small part of the general population starts to evacuate, your chances of vehicular movement with a significant amount of survival goods are about zero. As anyone who lives in the city knows, even a slight increase in traffic or disruption of flow brings everything to a halt. A 10 to 20 percent increase in outgoing traffic, combined with the inevitable accidents and breakdowns, will stop everything. This will be followed by panic, road rage, and chaos on the highways. Unless you head for the hills every time there's bad news, you probably will not beat the crowd.

For the purposes of this discussion, we will assume that the anticipated crisis will be so severe and extensive that (1) sheltering in place will not be an option and (2) outside help or rescue of any kind is unlikely.

Planning Your Evacuation

If driving your vehicle filled with survival and camping supplies is viable, you should definitely try it. To this end, you should have supplies in tote bins ready to load into your vehicle and go. Of course, you should never let your fuel tank get below half full, and if the conditions indicate that you may need to evacuate soon, keep the tank full. Every mile you can get by vehicle is one less that you will need to walk. Most people will head for the expressways and main roads, which will jam up quickly. Now is the time to use topographic road maps found at truck stops, Google Earth, and reconnaissance trips to locate back roads, side roads, alleys, and other drivable surfaces that may offer clear routes. Rivers, railroad tracks, and other features that cross your escape path will have only limited crossing points at bridges, underpasses, and tunnels. Try to get past these before they are closed off. Once these choke points are closed and the roads are blocked, you will have to abandon your vehicle and walk. You must be prepared for this eventuality.

All your main survival supplies must be in backpacks or wheeled carriers. Include sturdy hiking boots and all-weather clothing in your supply bins, and if water obstacles are anticipated, a canoe or inflatable raft as well. You may want to put a large bolt cutter in your vehicle for opening gates to service roads and shortcuts.

There are going to be a lot of less-prepared and more-desperate people out there, so being well armed will be a necessity. Getting through an urban area requires close-range volume of fire more than long-range accuracy. You need to quickly disable or suppress hostile fire while escaping the danger zone. Large-caliber, large-capacity handguns; short-barreled shotguns; and carbines are all effective. I also recommend carrying lots of smoke grenades to facilitate screening of movement. These are available at paintball supply outlets.

Escape Routes

Escape routes can make use of any unobstructed pathway that leads to a safer location. Out-of-the-box thinking is good for escape planning. Each city has a number of pathways cutting through the mass of built- up and populated terrain that can be used as escape routes. Refugees in the past have often used sewers, drainage systems, and even rooftops as escape routes. Anyone living in an area of closely packed homes and apartment buildings must have a ready knowledge of routes. Consider the following:

- Railroad tracks and abandoned right-of-ways offer unobstructed paths out of the city. In Chicago we planned to use these as our primary escape routes, but walking down tracks is not as easy as you may think. You have to focus on your footing and, of course, be alert for trains. Also, raised-rail embankments make you a silhouette for shooters, but trying to walk on the slanted side of the embankment is almost impossible. Still, they lead straight out of town and often have necessary bridges over obstacles.
- River and stream edges can offer routes, but they are often obstructed with vegetation that may make walking difficult. If you have or can find a boat or raft and have navigable waterways, they can offer a great way out of town.
- Power line paths are usually kept clear of obstructions and often have unpaved service roads underneath the wires. However, they seldom include ways for you to cross streams, rivers, and other obstacles.
- Bike paths and hiking trails and parkways are becoming more common in urban areas. Many of these are networked into systems that reach well outside the city. The survivor would be well advised to become thoroughly familiar with these and consider a bicycle as a primary or secondary evacuation system. Bikes are faster and can carry more gear than walking with a pack. Consider that a lot of others are going to use these obvious escape routes, so don't depend on them alone.
- Alleys are the preferred routes through built-up urban areas. Fences, trash containers, and garages offer plenty of cover and concealment while screening you from watchful eyes through many windows. Crossing streets from alley to alley is faster than at street corners, and alleys are less likely to be blocked or watched. Walking down the street or sidewalk is just not a good idea for survival evacuation if it can be avoided.
- Industrial areas will be pretty much abandoned in a general collapse. People don't live there, and looters will focus on shopping centers. So routing through such areas may be much safer than through residential and commercial zones.

This survival bike with a trailer for extra gear can go places a motor vehicle cannot and can carry more equipment than a backpack.

Working with Google Earth and taking hikes should help establish a number of alternative routes combining the above elements to get you out of the urban area.

Bivouacs and Hideouts

In the jammed traffic of an evacuation, you may make five to eight miles per hour before being forced to stop completely. The average person walks at about four miles per hour, but with your pack, zigzagging down paths and alleys, you will be lucky to make one to two miles per hour. It may take you several days to get out of the urban environment, so you need to consider safe places to hide and rest. Abandoned buildings, garages, and wooded areas may work for you. Underpasses and viaducts will probably attract too many others. Select locations off the main routes and paths that offer shelter without being too obvious.

Binoculars and Night Vision Gear

Two items that can give you a clear advantage in an urban escape are binoculars and night-vision equipment. A good pair of binoculars can let you see dangerous conditions and hostile individuals before you encounter them. Being prepared to deal with or avoid a problem ahead of time is a tremendous advantage. Night-vision gear gives you the option to move at night and still see threats ahead of you before they see you. Night movement with this ability can be much safer than daytime movement. In bivouac, you can see who's coming before they see you. These items are must investments if urban escape is a necessary part of your survival plan.

Alternative Plans

While survival fiction often paints the picture of a well-stocked retreat in the mountains, manned by a highly trained survival group, the reality is that most of us will have far more limited resources and may be limited to what we can carry to set up a camp once we are away from the city. Once automotive transportation is stopped and checkpoints are closed off, the amount of supplies you can carry will be severely limited. Backpacking, biking, and camping are advisable hobbies for every would-be urban survivor. Not everyone is able to carry a forty- to fifty-pound bug-out bag the twenty to forty miles that may be necessary to reach safety. Many families I know have adopted one of the two solutions below.

Solution #1: Store the majority of your survival supplies at a friend's house or in a self-storage unit well outside the city. You can then evacuate on foot if necessary with a basic survival pack and reach your supplies in a few days on foot or by bicycle. Some folks I know even store a second car at a remote location.

Solution #2: Have a hotel, motel, or campground that you like just beyond the city. If things look dangerous, take the family and your survival stuff on a mini-vacation there until things stabilize. You can still commute to work if necessary, but if things deteriorate, you have a head start on your escape.

CONCLUSIONS

Cities and closed-in suburbs are too densely populated to be sustainable once the infrastructure and civil services collapse. Lack of sanitation, water, food, and fire and police protection will rapidly lead to epidemics, riots, and famine. The city dweller must preplan a number of safe routes out of the area that minimize exposure. Physically scouting these routes ahead of time will offer the best chance of fast and effective evacuation to less hazardous locations. Having an evacuation pack and gear alone is inadequate without a thoroughly thought-out escape plan.

CHAPTER 3
Ten Items for the Prepared Home

Although you may or may not be at home when a disaster starts, you probably want to get there as soon as you can, if possible. First, we explore the decision of whether to stay home or evacuate. Next, we must consider the necessary items that are needed to survive in most home-based disaster situations.

STAY HOME OR RUN?

Men who had fought in several wars and many bloody battles told me that no horrors of a field of battle can be compared to the awful spectacle of the ceaseless exodus of a population, knowing neither the object of the movement nor the place where they might find rest, food, and housing . . ."

—Russian General Vasily Gourko

Premature or unnecessary evacuation may be the classic frying-pan-to-fire decision. Over my forty-five years as a survivalist, I have worked with dozens of survival groups developing both shelter-in-place and last-resort evacuation plans. During the Cold War, evacuation was the only option for the urban population while shelter in place was the best option for those outside the blast zones. Today's population faces a far more complex combination of disasters and disintegrations that make the decision of whether to stay home or evacuate more difficult. While staying home may be impossible in some situations, evacuation has considerable limitations and hazards that must be considered before taking to the road.

A great deal of survival-preparedness literature is devoted to evacuation plans, retreat development, and bug-out bags. While the ability to evacuate is a critical part of emergency preparedness, the assumption that evacuation should be the first choice in any survival scenario is (in my opinion) flawed. Placing all your hopes on getting to a retreat or cache with the limited supplies you can carry is a big gamble. At least half of the preppers I know lack the funds to fully stock both the home and any kind of retreat or large cache for extended survival periods. Many people have health issues, family obligations, or other factors that simply prohibit evacuation. Unless you and everyone in your family are in excellent physical condition and consistently engaged in backpacking, it is unlikely that you can carry a truly adequate bug-out bag very far if you are reduced to evacuation on foot.

Multi-family or group evacuation plans may look good on paper, but the complexity of travel, communications, and rendezvous under the chaotic conditions of a true national catastrophe may actually increase members' risks once they leave home. Premature evacuation may well increase the chances of injury, property loss, and exposure to the very hazards you are trying to escape. I have known survivalists who evacuated several times based on false information from panic peddlers and lost their jobs and homes as a result. Their obsession with evacuation *was* the disaster. Once you are on the road, you are dependent on just what you can carry and you are exposed to cold, heat, rain, fallout, epidemics, criminals, and all the hazards that you should be trying to avoid. Your chances of reaching any distant (one hundred miles or more) retreat are fifty-fifty at best.

Many catastrophes will develop slowly. In these cases, home-based adjustment, over years, may replace the need to panic and run. Critical needs—e.g., food, power, water, police protection—may decline and become unreliable. Developing the home as a base and networking with others to create alternative sources of critical supplies and services (e.g., water gathering, food production, community defense) may be a better survival plan than heading for the hills.

Of course, there are serious hazards to staying home as well. Your unprepared neighbors may gang up on you, fires may spread through the community, or roaming gangs may besiege you in your home. These hazards are greater in the urban and suburban areas, but these areas are equally more hazardous to evacuate from. Obviously such events as hurricanes, tornadoes, floods, and earthquakes that destroy or make your home and community untenable will require evacuation, but these are regional events where rescue and support services would be available within a day's walk and recovery would be anticipated.

The scenario that most preppers/survivalists anticipate is a massive and general catastrophe caused by an economic collapse, war, revolution, cyberattack, epidemic, or similar event. The idea that rural and wilderness regions offer more food and safety is highly doubtful. Edible crops in the field only exist for a short time near harvest, and farmers tend to shoot trespassers. Wild edibles, fish, and game can be had for a short while, but with unrestricted and inexperienced hunters and foragers roaming about, nothing will last long, and you may get shot before you catch anything. I am not saying that you should not have the skills and options necessary for evacuation. I am saying that evacuation has hazards and limitations that may outweigh the hazards of staying at home with your stored food, water, and weapons.

Unless you can afford to fully stock a retreat and are 100 percent sure you can get to it, your first preparedness priority is to be able to stay home, with enough food, water, medicines, and other critical supplies to stay off the streets completely for weeks or even months. This means not having to expose yourself to epidemics, gunfire, weather extremes, and other hazards. If you manage to ride out the first weeks of the situation at home, your chances of recovery and adjustment to the post-collapse society are much better than if you find yourself out in a distant region with dwindling supplies. In short, be able to run but be ready to stay.

Of course, many home emergencies must be handled at home without consideration of evacuation. Home fires, violent intruders, and severe storms are emergencies that require effective and immediate action at home. The ten categories of preparedness discussed below should provide a significant level of survival capacity in almost any emergency or disaster situation.

1. ITEMS IN THE BEDSIDE DRAWER

We spend about one-third of our lives in bed, so there is a 30 percent chance that the life-or-death emergency will strike while you are in bed. In that moment, everything will depend on what you can reach right away. Think about it. You wake up in the dark and the house is shaking from an earthquake, a bomb blast, or a tornado. You wake up in the dark and smell smoke or noxious fumes from a chemical incident. You wake up in the dark to the sounds of an intruder or the screams of your family. There is no time to get out your survival kit or look in your survival manual. You may suffocate, be trapped in the rubble, or be attacked in the next few seconds. You open the bedside drawer and find a bunch of junk!

First of all, only emergency items should be stored there. You don't want to be wasting precious seconds rummaging around for what you need. You should have two key items right on top of the bedside table: your cell phone and car keys should be placed there every night. Don't depend on a landline phone for emergencies. The landline phone may be dead when you need it most, and you cannot take it with you if you are forced to flee for safety. Your car keys should also be on the table. If all else is lost, at least your vehicle will be available and you can also use the button on the remote to set off your car alarm as another way to call for help. Imagine escaping into the night and realizing that you cannot use your vehicle and you do not have a phone!

SURVIVAL BEDSIDE NIGHTSTAND: Keys, cell phone, and wallet on top. Remember that cell phones do not automatically provide the 911 operator with your location as landlines do. So be sure and state that you are using a cell phone at the start of the call.

DRAWER: Large pepper spray, tactical flashlight, aspirin, Glock 23 with strobe light and laser pointer, N95 mask in plastic bag, whistle, and survival escape tool with gas valve wrench.

Here are some suggestions for what should be in the bedside drawer. You should have a good N95 dust mask in there. It will not protect you against poison gases and carbon monoxide from a fire, but it will offer some protection from soot, smoke, and hot air as you escape. It will also protect you from dust in a building collapse. Of course have a good flashlight. It should be one of the new LED lights that go a long way on a few batteries. Don't be cheap. The light may have to penetrate smoke and dust. It may be needed to signal rescuers to your location or to blind a would-be assailant. Make it bright and tough. You should also have one of those small, flat crowbars like the Stanley Wonder Bar or the combination hatchet, hammer, and pry bar survival tool to smash windows, open jammed doors, chop through plaster-board walls, and pry yourself out from under things. It's not a bad weapon either. If your family is spread out in the house, a whistle and walkie-talkies might be worth considering so you can activate the appropriate emergency plan.

If you are fifty years of age or older, you should keep a package of aspirin in that drawer. Many victims of heart attack wake up in the night with chest pain and don't survive long enough for help to get there. If you awaken with chest pain, swallow the aspirin immediately and call 911 on that phone you have right there. Your chances are now significantly improved.

Last, but not least, have a defensive weapon. If you have family members who come and go at odd hours, you may want a less-than-lethal first-response weapon, such as a police-size (200-gram) pepper spray or a Taser. The choice of lethal weaponry is up to you, but it must be reliable, handy, and easy to use. A .38-caliber revolver is one good, simple, and reliable choice. Anything in a good-quality .380-, .40-, or .45-caliber auto pistol should do well. In this case, you don't need to put out lots of high-velocity, high-penetration rounds. You need to stop one or two intruders in close quarters without shooting family members and neighbors in adjoining rooms or houses. If you wear glasses, keep them there along with your wallet.

These are items you will need to survive. You may want to throw in a few light sticks and a good knife to complete the bedside drawer, and you are ready when trouble comes in the night!

2. FIRE EXTINGUISHERS, SMOKE DETECTORS, AND CARBON MONOXIDE DETECTORS

When a fire starts in the home while you are asleep, you probably will not be able to put it out. Your only priority is to get out safely and immediately. The sound of a working smoke or carbon monoxide detector will give you just enough time to escape if you already have an escape plan and act quickly. You should have at least two carbon monoxide detectors and two smoke detectors or combination detectors. These should be in hallways, basements, and bedrooms. It is recommended that they be tested monthly and have batteries replaced at least annually. (See Chapter 2, "Ten Disasters to Prepare For.")

Under disaster conditions, the opportunities for a fire are greatly increased, while the availability of the fire department may be delayed or unavailable altogether. Even under normal circumstances, it takes at least five to ten minutes for fire departments to respond. Since fire doubles every one to two minutes, any fire that is not extinguished immediately is going to do significant damage. Do not be economical where fire extinguishers are concerned! Bigger is better. Having "almost" put out a fire will be of little comfort as your home burns down. Have large ABC-rated fire extinguishers throughout the home. Inspect them regularly for pressure. The larger commercial extinguishers can be tested and refilled at industrial safety services.

For class "A" fires—originating from wood, paper, dry grass, and similar materials—you can also use a common garden pump sprayer. These are good for extinguishing trash and brush fires but never flammable liquids or electrical fires. (See Chapter 2, "Ten Disasters to Prepare For.")

The two smaller, disposable extinguishers on the left may be okay for the vehicle or kitchen, but larger, refillable ten- and twenty-pound extinguishers are recommended for the garage, basement, and central closet.

Garden sprayers are good for class "A" fires. A very fine spray can retard a class "B" fire as a last resort only.

3. WATER AND FOOD SUPPLIES

"Water, water everywhere, and not a drop to drink" was the lament of the Ancient Mariner, becalmed and thirsty in a sea of undrinkable saltwater. Today water comes from a faucet or is purchased in bottles, clean and (arguably) pure. But what if it doesn't? Next to air, water is the most critical life-sustaining substance. The human body can survive much longer without food than without water. In the long term, you can't even produce and cook most foods without access to water. Your cleaning, decontamination, first aid, sanitation, and fire control also depend on water. (See Chapter 9, "Ten Ways to Gather and Purify Water.")

Food acquisition and storage are covered in some detail later in this book, but once the power

The repurposed containers on the left and the stackable container in the center store bleach-treated tap water. The folding water bottle behind the bleach bottle can be quickly added to the water store if a disaster is imminent. Filling bathtubs and even plastic bags in the minutes before the water goes off can increase your stores.

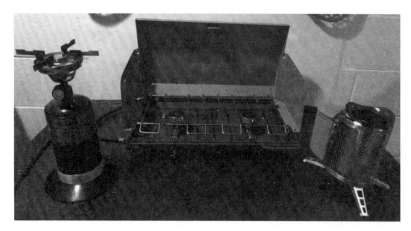

Left and center: A single-burner and twin-burner camp stove. Right: One of the new High-Tec rocket stoves. This one uses a battery-powered fan to blow air through burning twigs so effectively that you can heat a pot of water with just one or two handfuls. The heat also recharges the fan battery and can recharge a cell phone. It's still too dangerous and smoky for indoor use, but the fuel supply is nearly inexhaustible.

goes off, you will need to consume or preserve all fresh, refrigerated, and frozen foods within a short time. Having sufficient generator power to maintain refrigeration for a while will buy you more time to do this, but always assume that the power is not coming back. Consume perishables before using your nonperishable (e.g., canned, salted, dehydrated, freeze-dried) foods. You are going to need the capacity to cook and maybe can and dehydrate foods without normal sources of fuel and electricity. Fortunately, there are lots of great camping stoves available that use propane. In most weather you can also use propane (never charcoal) barbecue grills. They even make ovens that go over two-burner camp stoves. These are great for baking and drying. Solar ovens work for some applications and use no fuel, but take up a bit of space and, of course, depend on sunlight.

Don't forget to have a regular coffee pot to replace that now useless coffee maker. During a tornado a few years ago, my wife made it home from work through the downed trees and debris to find that I had hot coffee going on the camp stove.

4. SANITATION AND HEALTH NEEDS

In most long-term disasters, most people die from diseases that are caused and spread when sanitation systems fail. Human waste and garbage attracts insects and rats, breeds biological contaminants, and pollutes the air and water. Densely populated areas can become nightmares unless immediate and effective sanitation measures are instituted. Disposal of human waste and biological garbage will become a critical problem if the sewer systems shut down and garbage pickup is discontinued. A bucket with a plastic bag and bleach is one answer, or you can use one of the chemical toilets made for camping. Either way you may need to bury the bagged waste deep and far away if the situation lasts very long. Garbage can be burned if absolutely necessary, but it must be done well away from structures and brush fire hazards. Remember, the fire department isn't coming!

5. SHELTER AND WARMTH

Today's homes are energy dependent. They are designed to have a central air-conditioning and heating system. Heating them with limited fuel and small heaters is nearly impossible. You must consider closing off unnecessary rooms and eating, sleeping, and working in only one or two rooms throughout the cold season. The kitchen will be necessary for cooking, and a room large enough to accommodate everyone in sleeping bags can be sealed off and heated with a fireplace or space heaters. If unheated spaces actually get below freezing, any water pipes in them must be drained. If you have running water, you can let the faucets drip to prevent freezing or just heat the kitchen, bathroom, and basement to 40 degrees through the emergency. When pipes are allowed to

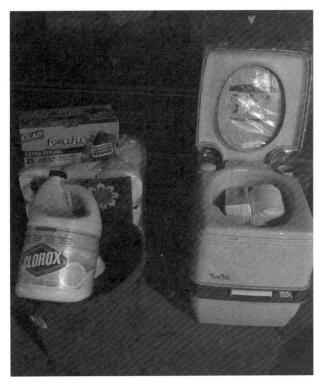

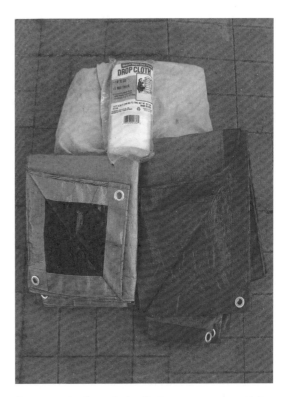

You can never have too much bleach, toilet paper, and heavy-duty plastic bags, and a chemical toilet is also a good investment. A survivor of the Siege of Leningrad stated, "It is good to have gold jewelry, but better to have toilet paper!"

Canvas, vinyl, and plastic tarps are essential home survival items.
Below: Shown left to right: kerosene heater (smelly), vented fireplace, and LP gas heater—all options for emergency heat.

freeze with water in them they will (1) stop the supply of water and (2) split and cause a flood once they thaw. Don't let that happen. In a prolonged situation, you may want to erect a tent in your living room for sleeping, as body heat will keep it warmer than sleeping in an open room. So you want to have sleeping bags, blankets, and LP gas-powered space heaters available. Better yet, have a heat-circulating fireplace and plenty of wood. In some cases your roof may be damaged or windows broken, so have plenty of tarps and tools on hand. (See item number nine, "Rescue Tools and Repair Supplies.")

6. EMERGENCY PLANS AND PACKS

The contents of evacuation packs and the larger bug-out or survival packs are covered in Chapter 5, "Ten Things You Should Have in Your Survival Pack(s)," so let's focus on planning here. It is human nature to avoid thinking about, much less planning for a disaster. But the old slogan that "if you're failing to plan, you're planning to fail" is doubly true for emergency plans when failure can be fatal. Not only must you acknowledge the potential for various disasters and emergencies, you must accept that you are responsible for being ready for them.

A great deal of attention is given to what equipment to have (e.g., survival kits) and to the specific skills (e.g., first aid, shelter building) needed for emergencies. Less attention is given to emergency planning principles and techniques. Government agencies and industries are required to maintain up-to-date emergency plans for every anticipated emergency. The responsible citizen and family would be well advised to make their own emergency plans for those situations that may endanger their lives and safety. Having the right emergency equipment and skills is important but having a plan for their effective and timely use is a key element in the preparedness triangle.

WHAT TO PLAN FOR?

Using some logical analysis and common sense, you should be able to select those emergencies that are the most likely to happen to you and would have the most serious consequences to your life, property, and freedom. These will differ for every individual and family. You may live in a high-crime area, an earthquake zone, or downwind of a chemical plant. You may work in a terrorist target zone, or you may have enemies with violent natures. If you smoke, a home fire is much more probable than a tornado to affect you. Consider the things that have happened in your area. What trends are developing in the areas where you live and work? It should be easy to come up with a number of emergencies for which you should have a plan.

Answering the Questions

Once you have a short list of potential emergencies, the process of planning for each one can begin. Emergency planning is the process of answering questions before Fate asks them. These questions are as follows:

- **WHAT events would trigger the plan?** It is critically important that everyone in the family or group understands that a certain event will trigger the plan without having to ask anyone. For example, the smoke detector going off, the lights going out, or hearing an intruder in the house should trigger immediate action by every member even if they are in different locations. You are at work while your wife is at home and the kids are at school. Suddenly there is a toxic chemical spill upwind of your home and the school. Each of you has to know what to do and hopefully where to meet when that trigger event happens. When event A happens, everyone executes his or her part of the plan for that occurrence.

- **WHAT actions are required in what order?** This is the most complicated part of the plan. You must cover all the critical actions but keep it simple and fast. The first element of the plan must be to stop or escape the immediate danger. This could be using a fire extinguisher, escaping from a home fire, taking shelter from a tornado, or calling 911. Gathering critical emergency items for continued survival would be next. You may need respirators, protective clothing, medical supplies, and weapons to stay alive. Having survived the immediate threat and provided protection against continuing hazards, your next priority is reaching your family and ensuring their continued safety. Having gathered loved ones and equipment, you can move on to long-term survival activities as needed. In the event of a home fire, escaping and gathering of the family are probably all that's needed. Surviving and escaping a civil disorder in your community would require a series of additional actions, such as preparing the home for defense, fire extinguishing, gathering survival packs, and following a preplanned route to safety.

- **WHERE will you be and where will you go?** Obviously, your location when disasters strike will greatly affect your planning. A plan to react to a nuclear, biological, or chemical (NBC) attack will be very different if you are at work or on the road than if you are at home. You also have to consider your primary shelter or escape destination and your main rendezvous location where you will meet others and access your survival equipment. You may have selected a number of temporary storm or blast shelters (e.g., culverts, basements) along your daily route. You can hang on in these with your small (carry-along) survival items for a few days and then make your way to your home or other long-term shelter. Never assume that everyone will be at home and have access to all your supplies when disaster strikes.

- **WHO is responsible for what actions?** In any emergency, it is critical that all members do their jobs. Who locks up the house? Who gathers the children? Who brings the supplies? Who calls 911? Who provides CPR? Make sure everyone can do each job (cross-train) if necessary, but clearly assign tasks.

- **WHEN to act and when to meet?** It could be hours or days before family or group members can move from the shelter, evacuate the danger area, and get to a designated assembly point or rendezvous. You should have several alternate meeting places and a time each day that members would be there. Your plan might say that you would meet at the abandoned gas station on a highway at noon four days after the trigger event and every day after that until all are assembled or ten days. If that location is unsafe (e.g., occupied, contaminated) the alternate location is the cluster of trees near the Wilson farm.

- **HOW will each action be achieved?** While some actions may be self-evident (e.g., run, hide, carry), some actions may require more detail. How to crawl out of a burning house or specifically what protective equipment to put on to protect against biological contamination may need to be included. Good training requires the minimum amount of detail included in the plan and offers flexibility.

- **WHAT if there are problems with the plan?** No plan survives the first few minutes of a disaster. Plan on things going wrong and try to have a plan that can get you past these inevitable problems. What if your route is blocked? What if you have to walk? What if you can't get to your survival pack? What if you have to evacuate? What if someone is injured? What if you or someone else cannot safely get home? You need alternate plans and backup equipment to deal with these inevitable challenges.

Emergency Plan Examples

Example 1: Home Fire

- **Trigger:** Smell smoke, see flames, smoke detector activated.

- **What Action:** Get to floor. Call 911. Test doors for heat before opening. Escape by crawling (route practiced) or through window. Get to neighbor's house (rendezvous). Direct fire department and inform them of missing family members. If the neighbors are not home, run to the convenience store on the corner.

Example 2: A Terrorist Attack Resulting in Civil Disorder

- **Trigger:** Terrorist nuclear attack occurs about one hundred miles upwind of your home, resulting in panic, riots, power failures, spreading fallout, and epidemics.
- **What Action:** All members access personal emergency and self-defense items. Put on best available respiratory and skin protection. Escape hazard areas if possible via railroad tracks, back roads, and other preplanned routes. If escape is not possible, take shelter (preplanned) in a location that minimizes exposure and is defendable or well concealed. When safe to do so, evacuate to home shelter. Person at home will establish shelter and defense, if possible, or evacuate with as much gear as possible to rendezvous point 1. If home has been abandoned, others will continue to rendezvous point 1 and meet there at noon each day until contact is made. Recover food, water, and medical supplies at rendezvous point 2 and establish shelter until emergency is over.

Of course, actual plans would probably include much more detail about the specific routes, equipment, and assignments, but all the basics are covered here.

Getting It Done

We play all kinds of video games and watch all kinds of highly unlikely adventure/survival videos while we put off real emergency planning and preparedness. Survival planning can be a game for the whole family that will be interesting and can save lives. A family planning session for a home fire, home invasion, tornado, or, yes, even "the big one" is time well spent.

Critical Equipment

Supplies and kits for home survival, as well as evacuation kits, are covered elsewhere in this book, but obviously the availability of equipment must be considered throughout the planning process. Your first plan must be made based on what you have at the time. Planning will probably highlight the need for additional items or the relocation of things you may need in a hurry. Plan to improve and then plan again.

Don't Guess — Know!

How long will it take to crawl blindfolded in smoke-filled rooms to your front door? Can you really build a filtered air shelter quickly enough in a biological attack? Can you really carry your survival gear five miles in an emergency? Test your equipment, practice your actions, and test your plan against worst-case scenarios. It has to be simple. It has to be practical. It has to work under the worst conditions.

Emergency Planning Tool

The following is a form you can use to guide your emergency planning efforts.

EMERGENCY PLANNING GUIDE

Emergency Situation (what is this plan for?): _____
_____
_____

Trigger Event (what event or events will cause this plan to be activated?) _____
_____
_____

Activation Code Word (optional) _____

EMERGENCY ACTIONS

ORDER/ PRIORTY	ACTIONS: BY WHOM? WITH WHAT? HOW?	NOTES / ALTERNATIVES
1		
2		
3		
4		
5		
6		
7		
8		
9		
10		

EMERGENCY ROUTES (INCLUDE MAPS IF NECESSARY)

FROM	TO	ROUTE DESCRIPTION AND ALTERNATES
Work	Home	
Work	Point #1	
Home	Point #1	
Point #1	Point #2	

MEETING PLACES AND RENDEZVOUS POINTS

NUMBER	LOCATION DESCRIPTION	TIME TO MEET
1		
2		
3		

NOTES: _____

_____

Plan reviewed (date)_____(Review at least annually)

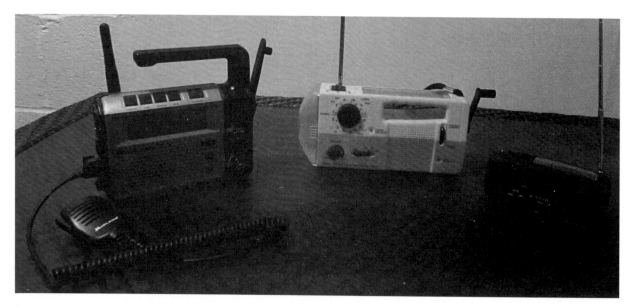

Emergency radios come in many forms. The one on the left is crank and battery powered, and has the capacity to transmit on the GMRS/FRS wavelengths. The center one has a light and a siren, and is crank and solar powered. The small radio on the right has a crank and solar power system, and can even be used to recharge your cell phone.

7. FIRST AID KIT AND MANUAL

In a massive disaster the emergency medical services (EMS) will be overwhelmed or even completely inoperative for extended periods. At the same time, the disaster itself and the attending efforts to survive will generate a high number of major and minor injuries. Illness from poor sanitation, stress, and lack of medications will also increase. Severe bleeding, infected wounds, shock, and heart attacks can result in death if not treated quickly. Fractures, dislocations, and other kinds of injuries will result in long-term or even permanent disability in the absence of effective first aid measures. Failure to learn first aid and have the necessary medical supplies on hand is inexcusable.

In addition to first aid training, you should have one or more good first aid manuals that go beyond short-term care instructions. Controlling bleeding; recognizing and treating shock; splinting; cleaning, managing, and closing wounds; and techniques for administering hydration and CPR are essential basic skills. Knowing how to move an injury victim from a dangerous area while minimizing discomfort and spinal injuries is also important. These should be covered in any true survival first aid manual. The contents of your first aid kit will depend much on the size of your family and the amount of skill you have. (See Chapter 8, "Ten Medical Skills You Should Know.")

The following is a minimum list if you want to make up your own kit.

Bandages and Supplies

- 50 assorted-size adhesive bandages
- 1 large trauma dressing
- 20 sterile dressings, 4x4 inch
- 20 sterile dressings, 3x3 inch
- 20 sterile dressings, 2x2 inch
- 1 roll of waterproof adhesive tape (10 yards x 1 inch)
- 2 rolls self-adhesive wrap, 1/2 inch
- 2 rolls self-adhesive wrap, 1 inch
- 2 rolls self-adhesive wrap, 2 inch
  - » 1 elastic bandage, 3 inch
  - » 1 elastic bandage, 4 inch
  - » 2 triangular cloth bandages
  - » 10 butterfly bandages
  - » 2 eye pads

Medications

- 2 to 4 blood-clotting agents
- 10 antibiotic ointment packets (approximately 1 gram)
- 1 tube of hydrocortisone ointment
- 1 tube of antibiotic ointment
- 1 tube of burn cream
- 1 bottle of eye wash
- 1 bottle of antacid
- 1 bottle syrup of ipecac (for poisoning)
- 1 bottle of activated charcoal (for poisoning)
- 25 antiseptic wipe packets
- 2 bottles of aspirin or other pain reliever (100 count)

- 2 to 4 large instant cold compresses
- 2 to 4 small instant cold packs
- 1 tube of instant glucose (for diabetics)

Equipment

- 10 pairs of large latex or nonlatex gloves
- 1 space blanket or rescue blanket
- 1 pair of chemical goggles
- 10 N95 dust/mist respirators or medical masks
- 1 oral thermometer (nonmercury/nonglass)
- 1 pair of splinter forceps
- 1 pair of medical scissors
- 1 magnifying glass
- 2 large SAM Splints (optional)
- 1 tourniquet
- Assorted safety pins

Optional Items If Trained to Use

- 1 CPR mask
- 1 bag valve mask
- 1 adjustable cervical spine collar
- 1 blood pressure cuff and stethoscope or blood pressure device
- 1 set of disposable oral airways
- 1 oxygen tank with regulator and non-rebreather mask
- Suturing kit and sutures
- Surgical or super glue

If you have advanced training, such items as a suturing kit, IV setup, and medical instruments may be added.

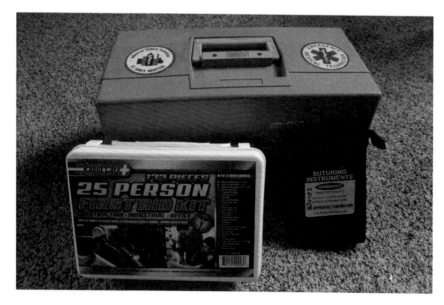

You can build your own first-aid kit in a tackle-box (rear) or buy one. This twenty-five-person industrial kit is sold at hardware stores and is reasonably priced and well stocked for injuries. Specialized kits like the one for suturing can be added as your skill level increases.

8. EMERGENCY LIGHTS AND POWER

While we take the availability of electricity and natural gas for granted, both are dependent on vulnerable and fragile delivery systems. Earthquakes, tornadoes, and other natural phenomena can disrupt these systems for lengthy periods. Solar flares, cyberattacks, electromagnetic pulses (EMP), and terrorist actions can disable the electrical supply grid for months or longer. Even an epidemic or civil disorder that keeps workers away from generating stations and other critical facilities could result in the shutting down of these systems. The extended interruption in electrical power would have catastrophic effects on water pumping, fuel supplies, and medical facilities. Civil disorder would break out in urban areas within one or two days. You will need to be able to sustain your own minimal energy needs while keeping a low profile. Having that noisy generator running and your house lit up is an invitation to unwanted guests. It would be best to cover windows and keep lights to a minimum and in the basement or back rooms when possible.

Emergency Power

Depending on your budget and priorities, you can have a power and heating system that totally replaces outside sources, or you can scale down to candles and a stove or fireplace. Most folks will opt for something in between. Keep in mind that in a truly large-scale, long-term disaster, natural gas, propane cylinders, gasoline, and other fuel will eventually be unavailable. So you may have a tier-one system of generators and gas heaters and a tier-two system of solar-powered, wood-burning, and candle-lit living. Do not be dependent on just one method for power and heating, or on one type of fuel.

Generators

Large, natural gas–powered generators are efficient and popular. They offer seamless switching to alternative power and enough power to run all appliances and lights, but they may be too expensive or impractical for many. The next alternative is a smaller portable gasoline generator. These come in a variety of sizes and power outputs. They need to be run periodically, and the gasoline should be changed at least annually to ensure that they will run when you need them. In most towns, there are limits on how much fuel you can store. Always store flammables away from the house in safety cans and in steel cabinets.

Note: In many cases the gas supply will continue even when the electricity is off. Having an electrician wire your furnace so that the fan and controls can run off your generator is well worth the expense.

The 100-watt generator on the right is easy to move and uses little fuel. I ran my sump pump and small freezer alternately on this for two and a half days on a few gallons of gas, but, of course, I had to rely on solar lamps and candles for lights. The larger 3,500-watt generator can power most home appliances but burns a lot of fuel in the process.

The older-style flashlight at top has the advantage of being a weapon if needed. On the left is a solar-rechargeable flashlight. You can just leave these in the window, and they will always be ready. In the center is a small headlamp that is very handy for getting around and doing work in a dark home. At right is a high-powered tactical flashlight you must have accessible at all times. You can use a solar panel to recharge all the batteries.

Emergency Light

When the lights go out, the first thing you reach for is a flashlight. Don't be stingy about your home flashlights—have them handy in most rooms. In the first few minutes of an emergency, you need to see and be seen. These flashlights should be sturdy and powerful. Your primary flashlight should be no less than 350 lumens, but the more the better. Multiple small flashlights around the house can get you to your main flashlights and lanterns safely, but the one in the bedside drawer should always be a powerful one. Some or all of your lanterns and flashlights should be solar/rechargeable. A solar battery recharger is recommended as well.

Above right: Beyond the flashlights, you have lots of options for light (left to right): LP gas, kerosene, candles, battery, and crank. At center is a glow sheet that gives usable light after charging in the sun. New solar-powered lanterns are highly recommended.

These kerosene lamps can replace electric lights, functioning as they did in the nineteenth century. You will want to have plenty of spare parts and mantels (center) in stock.

9. RESCUE TOOLS AND REPAIR SUPPLIES

You may be buried in your own home or need to rescue your family or neighbors. You may also need to clear streets for escape or dig out essential supplies and materials. In such cases, heavy tools may suddenly be critical to survival.

A few decades ago everyone did their own repairs and had a good selection of tools on hand. Some folks still do, but a lot of us don't. There are some heavy tools that are particularly important in an emergency where cutting, lifting, prying, chopping, digging, and smashing are required. Axes, hatchets, saws, and even chainsaws are necessary to remove fallen trees and heavy debris. A selection of small and large crowbars is essential to rescue and self-rescue. A small and a large sledgehammer really come in handy to smash through walls and debris piles. Have at least one good auto jack or hydraulic hand jack to move heavy objects. A come-along and lots of extra heavy rope for pulling very heavy objects are also handy.

Repair Tools and Supplies

In addition to rescue and debris-removal tools, you need to have enough tools and materials to make temporary repairs to your home. Many kinds of disasters can leave your home with a damaged roof, broken windows, and other damage that will let in

Rescue and self-rescue tools. These are best kept in your shelter spot since you may have to dig yourself out.

51

I have moved objects weighing many tons using hydraulic jacks and come-alongs. Such devices impart huge advantages in survival and rescue situations.

A few home repair tools. Have enough tarps and heavy-duty plastic to cover broken windows and damaged roofing. You should have plenty of rope, wire, tape, and nails as well.

cold, rain, and wind. A basic tool set of hammers, saws, pliers, and screwdrivers is a must. Stock up on heavy-duty plastic sheeting and tarps to cover roofs and windows.

A selection of nails in various sizes is important. You will need lots of duct tape, strong rope, and heavy wire as well. You may also want to consider having chicken wire to cover the outside of windows to deflect thrown or blown objects.

10. SELF-DEFENSE WEAPONS

The choice of home-defense weapons is subject to endless controversy. I know a few people who still have no firearm at home because they are constantly confused by the conflicting recommendations of "experts." One of the problems is that "experts" are professional shooters and shooting trainers, whereas the great majority of those needing a gun for self- and home-defense are not. Most working family people will have limited budgets, time, and opportunities to practice with and maintain their firearms. Having an arsenal of high-cost and high-maintenance arms that you can become expert with is certainly desirable but seldom practical for most people.

I will confine my recommendations here to practical, reliable, and affordable firearms for home-defense, not street use. In all cases, the owner should take a basic training course and practice on a range with each firearm at least once each year. Certainly, if you can afford the time and money, take a full-fledged armed self-defense course. Most important, handle, store, and use firearms safely. If children live or visit your home, every firearm must be locked up. Children are very good at finding things that are hidden and can usually figure out how to load an unloaded gun. Don't take chances.

Survival Shotguns

If you are going to have just one gun for home use, get a shotgun. We hear a lot about the handguns and rifles that are recommended for home-defense and survival, but the shotgun is usually overlooked—even though it may be the best and most versatile survival weapon of all. Granted, it's not easy to conceal and it's hard to employ in tight spaces, so it's not ideal to foil street crime or carjacking. However, for home-defense and urban and suburban civil-disorder situations, the shotgun has great advantages over handguns and carbines.

Just the sight of that big barrel and the sound of a round being jacked into the chamber can be enough to discourage most thugs. One shot puts multiple projectiles downrange in a pattern that has a much better chance at a first-shot hit than any other firearm. A direct hit at close range will stop the criminal in his tracks. Sending dozens of projectiles downrange will stop a whole gang. Lower-velocity "law enforcement" rounds are ideal for close-quarter and indoor encounters since they have reduced recoil and less likelihood of injuring innocent people farther away. In the street, you are getting off about six rounds to the handgun's one or two. Shotguns have amazing versatility. You can perforate a vehicle with buckshot or stop it with a slug or armor-piercing round. You can use breaching rounds to open doors or use exploding or incendiary rounds to discourage attackers or clear your escape route. Of course, once you are safe, you can still bring down game for food with shot and slugs. As a bonus, compared to handguns and combat rifles, shotguns are relatively cheap. You can get a new combat-style pump shotgun for $300 to $400. Plus, shotguns are often less regulated than handguns and rifles and attract less attention.

I do recommend that you replace the stock with a folding or collapsible stock for close situations. You may also want to add a shell holder for quick reloads or to keep special rounds handy. Other customizing options include a magazine extension, barrel shroud, and flashlight and laser pointer. Accessories are available for most Mossberg, Winchester, and Remington shotguns from most sporting goods stores.

Home Survival Handguns

Handguns for concealed carry are addressed in Chapter 6, "Ten Ways to Avoid and Survive Street Crime." Handguns can double as first-access home-defense weapons, though you may want to consider large-capacity and larger-caliber handguns for home-defense. Modern semiautomatic pistols are the most common choice for home defense. They are reliable and safe, and give the defender multiple shots. They also can be fitted with lights and laser pointers to blind the intruder and ensure accurate shooting. The Glock shown in the bedside drawer in this chapter is typical of this type.

Above left: A wide variety of ammunition is available for all occasions. Shown here: law enforcement (short), double-ought buckshot, slugs, armor-piercing, flamethrower, fireball, breaching, and nonlethal rubber rounds.

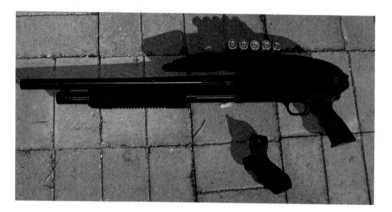

Above: This Mossberg 500 twelve-gauge "camper" model came with a pistol grip (no stock), which was easily replaced with a folding stock and a five-round shell holder.

Ithaca "riot gun" designed for police use outdoors. It's a little less maneuverable indoors and not as convertible, though you could saw off the stock and refinish the pistol grip.

Revolvers still have many advantages and deserve serious consideration. Revolvers were the original "automatic" handguns, able to fire multiple rounds without reloading. They remained popular with police and the military even after the introduction of reliable autoloading pistols, such as the Colt .45, model 1911, and the Walther

PPK. Large-frame revolvers, such as the Colt Python, firing .38 Special and .357 Magnum ammunition, and various brands of revolvers firing the powerful .44 Magnum round remained in use by highway patrolmen and outdoor guides well into the 1980s. And, of course, there was a certain Inspector Callahan (Clint Eastwood) of the San Francisco Police Department and his famous .44 Magnum.

The introduction of the Glock and other modern, reliable autoloaders with their high-capacity magazines and durable composite frames resulted in a shift away from revolvers. Today revolvers are considered bulky and outdated by many. Admittedly, even the lightest "air-weight" revolvers are less-concealable than the new compact 9mm and .380-caliber autoloaders. But in situations where concealability and weight are less important than reliability and stopping power, large-caliber revolvers deserve serious consideration. Let's consider their comparative qualities in relation to survival and home self-defense applications.

- **Ammunition capacity:** Although most autoloaders have eight- to seventeen-round magazines and can be reloaded quickly, the reality is that your first few shots are usually the most important in a close-encounter, survival/defense situation. Here the absolute reliability and power of those first six to eight rounds is more important than the unlikely event of an extended ten to fifty round gun battle. Most older revolvers were limited to six rounds (six-shooter), but modern revolvers in .357-caliber can be found with seven- and even eight-round cylinders. The Smith & Wesson Model 617 holds seven rounds and the Taurus Model 608 holds eight rounds, whereas most .44-Magnum revolvers are limited to five or six rounds. Eight rounds of .357 should do the trick! There are speed loaders and half-moon clips that can reload fairly quickly and even one-handed reloading techniques.

This sturdy stainless-steel revolver can fire eight .38-caliber or .357 rounds and has a contoured rubber grip and ported barrel to improve accuracy.

- **Power:** While the debate goes on regarding the effectiveness of various (e.g., 9mm, .40 S&W, .45 ACP) autoloader rounds, there is little question about the effect of a .357 or .44 Magnum round. A few very expensive and bulky automatics fire comparable rounds.

- **Accuracy:** The weight and simplicity of the action, combined with larger sights, actually make shooting large-caliber revolvers easier than shooting automatics. I would not recommend anything shorter than a four-inch barrel in these weapons. Several models come with ported barrels that further reduce muzzle climb and recoil. Many of these revolvers come with rubberized contoured grips that establish consistent hand position.

- **Dependability:** This is a primary requirement for any survival weapon: it must work every time under any conditions with little or no maintenance. Here is where the revolver really excels. The old adage "six for sure" (maybe seven or eight) means that even an untrained person with a poorly kept revolver can depend on getting off every round. Of course, you should practice with your weapon and keep it clean, but revolvers are easy to clean without the need for disassembly, and they are easy to operate. They are available in stainless steel, and this option should always be your choice.

- **Selection:** You are not looking for a refined match-grade pistol for competition or show. What you want here is a tough, reliable, and affordable weapon that will fire that big round at the threat with your adrenaline-powered fingers squeezing (probably pulling) the trigger. While the .44 Magnum is a great round, the .357 Magnum is certainly powerful enough, offers greater capacity, and can fire the more economical and common .38 Special for practice.

Conclusion

Large-caliber revolvers offer clear advantages in power and reliability, and are at least comparable in accuracy. Although autoloaders are less bulky and can hold a larger number of rounds, these advantages are not always the most important in a survival/combat situation. Autoloaders have advantages when conceal-ability or sustained battle capacity is required, but the large-caliber revolver is still superior in many situations and should be included in your survival battery.

Rifles and Carbines

Rifles and carbines are a poor choice for in-home defense. Even with shorter barrels and collapsible stocks, they are hard to maneuver in rooms, and their high-velocity bullets can go through multiple walls to injure others inside or even outside the home. Shotguns are effective for close defense against exterior threats as well, but if you anticipate multiple assaults from long range or you are likely to need to evacuate through combat-zone envi-ronments, a combat-style rifle may be a good

An M16 clone with a collapsible stock and a reflex combat sight on the top rail.

investment to supplement your shotgun and handgun choices. Obviously bolt-action, small-caliber rifles used for hunting and target shooting are unsuitable for these situations. Exploring all the choices would require a whole book, but the most popular choices are the wide variety of rifles based on the military AR-15 in 5.56/.223 calibers and the ubiquitous Russian-designed AK-47 and its clones firing 7.62x39mm ammunition. Both are available in a wide variety of designs. The M16 rifle variants have rails that can accommodate a wide variety of accessories, including specialized sights, lights, and pointers. In general, the AK-47 is a bit more robust and requires less maintenance, but it is less accurate at longer ranges than the AR-15s. There are way too many vari-ables to make specific recommendations here, but this is not a good item to buy cheap or used. If you seriously anticipate needing this kind of firepower, you need to invest in several extra high-capacity magazines and lots of ammunition.

An AK-47 clone with a folding stock (away from view) and a spare magazine.

Rules for Safe Storage and Use of Defensive Firearms

- Even when you are *sure* that the firearm is not loaded, keep the muzzle pointed in a safe direction away from any people. Remember that a bullet can go through walls and furniture to strike people in other locations.
- Keep your finger off the trigger until you actually intend to shoot. Position your trigger finger outside the trigger guard.
- Firearms not designated for emergency defense should be unloaded when not actually in use.
- Know your firearm. Always read the manual, know how to safely open and close the action, and know how to safely remove any ammunition from the firearm and its magazine or cylinder. Know how to tell when it's loaded or unloaded.
- Store firearms in a locked cabinet, safe, or gun vault when not in use. A quick-access, combination-locked gun case can be used for emergency defense weapons.
- Store your ammunition in a locked location separate from firearms.
- Use a gun-locking device that renders the firearm inoperable when not in use.
- Make sure young people in your home are aware of and understand the safety guidelines concerning firearms.
- Always unload, clean, and place your firearms in their secure storage location immediately after returning from a hunting trip or a day at the range. Do not leave them lying around where they can cause an accident.
- When using your firearm in the home for self-defense, be absolutely sure that no family member is in the line of fire or in an adjoining room.
- When using your firearm in the home for self-defense, be absolutely sure of your target. Clearly identify the target as an intruder and not a family member. Panic shooting and shooting in the dark or through doors can have tragic consequences.
- Be sure to tell the police of your location in the house and that you are armed when you call 911.
- If an intruder is in the house, do not go looking for him. Call 911 and take up a defensive position until the police arrive.
- When police arrive, immediately put down your weapon and keep your hands visible. Don't be mistaken for the threat.

Summary: Ten Things You Must Have at Home for Emergencies

1. Water and bleach
2. Emergency food supplies and stoves
3. First aid kit and manual
4. Alternative lighting and heat
5. Alternative power
6. Fire extinguishers
7. Emergency radio (AM/FM/WX/GMRS)
8. Tools and repair supplies
9. Established emergency plans
10. Self-defense weapons

CHAPTER 4
Ten Items You Should Always Carry

"It's not what you have. It's what you have with you. It's not what you can do. It's what you do."

Let's face it, you are not going to be carrying a survival pack or kit with you most of the time and in many cases you will not be able to access your primary survival supplies immediately. In many situations, your ability to survive the first minutes or even hours of a disaster will depend solely on what you know and what you have in your pockets. Since most of the items listed are relatively inexpensive, you should just preload them into every jacket or vest that you have. In the summer, when you are not wearing jackets or vests, you may need to put them into your cargo pants or shorts pockets. The following items can get you through many short-term emergencies. Empty pockets are an invitation to becoming a victim.

1. SMALL POCKET KNIFE

There is probably no single item that defines, establishes, and sustains an individual's survival, self-reliance, and freedom potential more than the knife. The knife and its modification, the spear, were in use long before the arrow, sling, or firearm. Flint blades predate almost any other man-made device. The term "Saxon" in Anglo-Saxon comes from the name of the long, heavy-bladed knife, called the *seax*, carried by the Anglo-Saxons. Carrying the *seax* was the mark of a free man. Slaves, of course, were prohibited from carrying arms. As we know, being prohibited from carrying is synonymous with oppression. The possession of a knife of any kind gives you a tremendous advantage in almost any survival situation. Don't leave home without it!

You may want to have a small, low-priced knife in every jacket to ensure that you always have at least one knife, but you should have a high-quality knife that you keep with your daily carry items (e.g., wallet, keys, cell phone). You may be able to carry a large folding blade in casual clothing, but have a smaller pocket knife for dress-up. Cargo pants usually have a pocket that fits a three-inch folding knife. Carrying a Swiss Army knife or multi-tool on your belt is the best option for casual dress. While the multi-tool devices are handy, the Swiss Army knives are better at being knives first and tools second. Don't go cheap for your primary carry knife, but don't get fooled into paying too much just for a brand name.

Note: Before 9/11, I wore my Swiss Army knife on planes all the time. Of course, you cannot carry a knife on a plane anymore, and even carrying a nonmetallic blade is risking serious issues, but you can put one in checked luggage to have once you reach your destination. Just be sure to remove it from your pockets before checking your bag. The Transportation Security Administration has a huge collection of knives taken from travelers.

The multi-tool (upper left) has lots of applications, but the Swiss Army knife (far right) functions better as a knife. Both can be carried on a belt without attracting attention. The two smaller knives (top center) are for smaller pockets. The three-inch folding-blade knife (bottom) fits in large pockets but may be illegal or attract too much attention. It is preferable to the smaller knives if you can carry it.

2. FIRE STARTERS (MATCHES, LIGHTER, AND STRIKER)

Here again you want to have some kind of fire starter in every coat pocket. Even a book of matches or a lighter is better than nothing. If you go with matches, just put them in a plastic bag. Waterproof, windproof camp matches are better yet. I have had cheap Zippo lighters that worked fine after four years in a pocket. You can add small magnesium fire strikers, which can be purchased for less than two dollars. Strikers are reliable but require some skill and time, whereas matches and lighters provide a flame immediately. You may want to have both.

Lighter, camp matches, and magnesium fire starter.

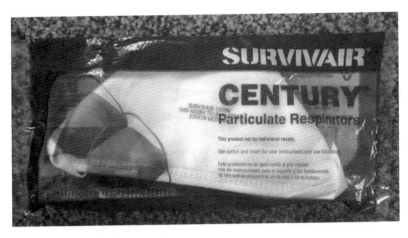

A dust/mist mask like this one can be a true life-saver in many disasters. Some of the people fleeing from the World Trade Center on 9/11 were seen wearing these because they had experienced the earlier bombing in New York City.

3. MINIATURE LED FLASHLIGHT

These micro flashlights come in a variety of sizes. I recommend that you have one on your key chain and another one in every coat pocket. I have 1-LED minilights in lighter jackets and 4-LED lights in parkas and coats. Even the smallest LED light gives you a big advantage when the lights go out in the elevator or anywhere else.

4. FOLD-FLAT N95 DUST/MIST MASK

If you can't breathe or are breathing toxic material, your chances of survival go way down. Carry a N95 fold-flat dust/mist respirator. These can be purchased at any hardware store and provide protection against most biological agents, toxic particulates, and mists, as well as limited and temporary protection from toxic chemicals. But they do not protect wearers from carbon monoxide or other toxic gases. A variety of man-made and natural disasters will produce smoke, soot, toxic dusts, and vapors. Having respiratory protection in your pocket is a must.

5. WHISTLE

Disasters are noisy. There is crashing, blowing, burning, screaming, and yelling. A piercing whistle has a much better chance of getting attention than your voice. Whistles are cheap and small, so you have no excuse for not always having one.

6. SELF-DEFENSE DEVICE (FIREARM OR PEPPER SPRAY)

Pepper spray devices are cheap and small enough for every key chain and pocket. Even if you carry a handgun, you should have options. I don't include Tasers here because they are larger and require close contact, but if you have room in your pockets, that's an option. Handguns are certainly the best choice for personal defense on the streets. While most states allow some kind of open or concealed carry, I prefer concealment in all cases. Since the criminal or terrorist is going to initiate the violence, we can assume that he will shoot any armed persons he spies before they can react. Let the terrorist be surprised, and not you. The size of your carry gun depends somewhat on your ability to conceal it, but you certainly want to have stopping power and at least six shots.

Full-sized handguns are generally difficult to conceal and unnecessarily bulky for constant carrying. Remember, you're carrying the weapon to stop an attack or facilitate your escape, not to fight a war.

If you are going to carry a concealed firearm regularly, you will need a variety of carry devices and probably more than one size of weapon. There are plenty of good inside-the-belt and outside-the-belt fast-draw holsters that can secure your weapon out of sight under a loose T-shirt or jacket. There are also some great concealed-carry vests and jackets available. In warmer weather or casual situations (no jackets), it is difficult to conceal a firearm in a belt holster of any kind. You probably need to consider having an enclosed belt pouch or belted holster pouch. If asked what's in there, I just say "a wireless hand-held device." While pocket carry is not the best option, it sometimes is the only one. In such cases I carry a small six-shot .380-caliber.

The small .38-caliber revolver on the upper left may be old school and a bit bulky, but it is absolutely reliable. The small-frame Glock (upper right) carries 9x9mm rounds and is still easy to conceal in most cases. The small Walther .380 caliber (bottom left) is more concealable and holds seven rounds. The very small 4-shot, .22-caliber Sharps derringer (bottom right) is ultra-concealable but does not have much stopping power. Still, it is way better than nothing.

Concealment options. The leather concealed-carry vest and the canvas vest on top provide comfortable access to large- and medium-sized firearms. The concealed carry pouch can be worn comfortably with summer clothing. Other pouches are available that go directly on your belt.

automatic padded with a few bandanas for comfort and to avoid outlining its shape. Although anything smaller than .380 caliber is of doubtful value in self- defense, it is far better than nothing. So a smaller caliber is an option when concealment is difficult.

7. FIRST AID ITEMS

If you are dependent on medication of any kind, you should carry some with you at all times. You may be unable to get home or reach a pharmacy for a length of time during a major emergency. Heart medications, insulin, asthma medication, epinephrine for allergies, and other emergency or daily medications must be handy at all times. While you can't carry a full first aid kit around with you, a few items will come in handy or even prove lifesaving in an emergency. If you are more than fifty years old, carrying a packet of aspirin at all times is important. Taking aspirin at the first sign of a heart attack can mean the difference between life and death. A few Band-Aids are handy for small cuts or repairs. A miniature bottle of alcohol-based hand sanitizer can clean wounds, prevent infections, and be used as a fire starter in an emergency. Depending on pocket space, you may want to carry a small tourniquet or blood-stopper packet, but a bandana can be used almost as quickly. (See the section on arterial bleeding in Chapter 8 of this book.)

Top row: RAT tourniquet and bandana that can be used with a stick as a tourniquet.
Bottom row: SWAT-T tourniquet, blood-stopper gauze, and military CAT tourniquet

8. BANDANA

You can just stuff some napkins into your pockets to provide an emergency wound cover, fuel for a fire, and dust mask over your mouth, or you can include a large handkerchief or bandana. The bandana is my recommendation. Bandanas were a must-have in past centuries and should be carried by anyone seeking to be perpetually self-reliant today. Bandanas come in a variety of colors and usually are about 22x22 inches square, costing less than three dollars each. They can easily be folded into any pocket. A bandana can be quickly turned into an effective bandage, tourniquet, splint/sling, dust mask (not nearly as good as the folding N95 mask, but far better than nothing), head cover, short rope, carrying sack, help flag, and more. MacGyver could probably find another 100 uses for it. Oh, and don't forget its use as a cleaning cloth and handkerchief. I recommend that you carry two, one red or yellow and the other dark or camouflage.

9. MEDICAL INFORMATION CARD

In an emergency, you may be seriously injured or incapacitated. In such cases, rescuers, medics, and others may need critical information in order to provide effective care and to contact your family. You should always carry a bright orange or red card in a visible place on your person or in your wallet. A sample is shown below.

FRONT	BACK
EMERGENCY CONTACT AND MEDICAL INFORMATION	MEDICAL INFORMATION
In Emergency Contact: Wilma Johnson **Phone:** (444) 555-9123 **Doctor contact:** Dr. Jack Hansen / St. Mary's Hospital **Phone:** (444) 555-0005	**Medical Conditions:** Diabetic, Stroke 1/20/2014 **Medications in Use:** Insulin injectable, aspirin **Blood type:** B-Positive **Allergic to:** Sulfa

10. SPECIAL ITEMS AND SUBSTITUTIONS

There are dozens of pocket survival kits, cards, and gadgets on the market. Some combine whistles, flashlights, compasses, and magnifiers. (Survival cards are generally flat, sharpened, cut-out pieces of stainless steel that serve various survival functions.) These can be used to replace some but not all of the items listed above or as backup pocket or vest items.

CLOSING NOTES

I am aware that some folks think that having an app on a cell phone covers some of these needs, and that's okay for backup. But technology can never be as reliable as actual tools and supplies, and these devices and the help they are supposed to bring are likely to fail just when you need them most. Real will always beat virtual.

Now you're ready for anything, anytime, anywhere. You are perpetually prepared and self-reliant, the go-to person in any emergency. You can save yourself in that first few minutes of an emergency and help others. This should make you feel good about yourself every day.

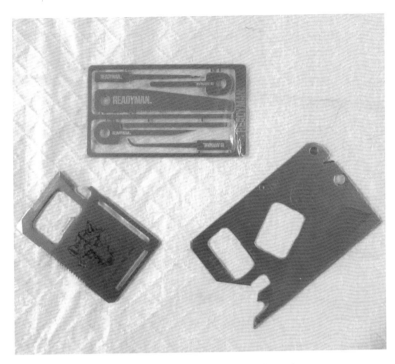

Survival cards perform specialized survival functions.

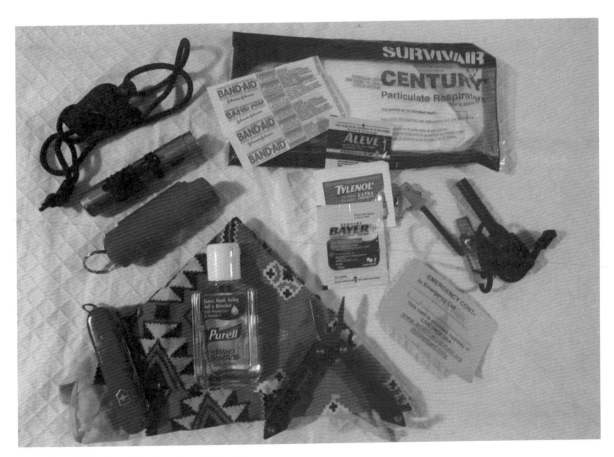

A pocket full of survival and confidence!

CHAPTER 5
Ten Things You Should Have In Your Survival Pack(s)

What should be in the survival pack, evacuation pack, or bug-out bag is the subject of countless articles and lectures, but there continues to be a demand for guidance as new "survivalists" and "concerned citizens" seek to become more prepared. Having some emergency stuff scattered about the house is just an indication that you are worried, but having a complete survival pack is proof that you are ready for whatever happens.

With the great variety of man-made and natural-disaster potentials increasing every year, failure to have a survival pack is inexcusable and irresponsible. The survival pack provides the ability and means to live and operate independently of the social and economic system for extended periods. Although this may never be necessary, the very existence of this pack confers a state of independence and liberation on its owner. The owners of survival packs have certified their responsible citizenship by their actions. These are the people who will not need to panic or become criminals in order to survive a disaster or hard times. These are the folks who will have the best chance to survive and help their neighbors. The well-stocked and organized survival pack is an insurance policy and a declaration of independence that is well worth the investment.

I have been developing and modifying my survival pack since the age of about twelve (long story). That's over sixty years and dozens of modifications to get the recommendations below.

PACK SELECTION AND PLACEMENT

The reality is that most people will never actually carry their packs very far. In most cases they will open it up and use the contents while remaining in their homes or nearby shelters through an emergency. It may be carried only a few blocks to a safer location or thrown into the family vehicle for the drive to safety. But you should prepare it for the worst-case situation, where it must be carried on the back for miles and provide at least the minimum survival needs under all anticipated hazards to life.

I have seen people with packs they could barely lift, much less carry. I have seen people who needed medical attention after trying to carry their packs a few miles on a test hike. If you are in the military or you are a frequent backpacker, you can probably carry fifty-plus pounds of gear, but average citizens will need to keep the pack weight down to twenty to thirty pounds maximum if they are going to cover any distance without exhaustion or injury. Supplemental food, shelter, and equipment can be kept in duffle bags next to the survival pack to be used in stay-at-home or vehicle-transported situations, but the pack alone must provide for all needs (e.g., water, food, shelter, medical) for three to five days. I do not recommend an oversized pack since you will be tempted to fill it up. A pack that is about twenty inches high, ten inches wide, and eight inches thick, with plenty of side pockets and padding, should hold about eighteen to twenty-five pounds of gear and supplies.

The pack should include external tie-downs or straps to attach a blanket or light sleeping bag, as needed. Zipper pockets and gear clips on the waist belt and shoulder straps are recommended for keeping items you need to get to quickly. The color depends on the area you will be surviving in. A camouflage pack may be normal in some environments, but may attract attention in others. Black, brown, or dark gray are recommended alternatives.

Inconspicuous survival packs kept handy in a closet. The wheeled luggage on the left also has shoulder straps to carry as a pack. The smaller pack is more appropriate for short-term evacuations.

Survival pack nestled in a large tote bin. Note the sneakers and firearms with magazines in the bin. This provides waterproof protection and instant grab-and-go availability.

Good-quality packs of the kind described above cost from $75 to $150. If you cannot afford that much, check out military surplus stores. The Better than Nothing (BTN) rule applies to all survival equipment. The

BTN rule is that if you cannot find or afford the ideal item, then get the best you can because anything is better than nothing when it comes to survival. You can probably get an "adequate" pack for twenty to forty dollars.

I also recommend that you keep your survival pack inside a plastic tote bin when not in use. This protects it from all kinds of hazards, including dirt, water, pests, and curious hands. The tote bin can also contain supplemental belt and pocket items that will go with the pack, such as knives, firearms, field clothing, canteens (kept full), and energy bars.

Unless you live alone, you will need to assemble packs for each family member above the age of ten. You may need to carry supplies for younger children yourself. These packs should have all the essentials (e.g., water, shelter, food, medical, sanitation, clothing) that your pack has but does not need to duplicate things like stoves, water purifiers, and tools. Therefore, they can have extra food and shelter items.

Where you keep the pack is important. If your garage burns down, you still have the supplies in your house, but if your house burns down or cannot be accessed, you will really need your pack. So maybe you want to keep the pack or a second pack in a shed, garage, or other location separate from your house. That's up to you.

Belt and Pocket Items

These are items that would not normally be carried inside the pack, but you would need to have with you if you use the pack. These items should be stored right alongside the pack in a bag, so you can quickly grab them as you put on the pack and then put them on your belt or in your pockets as soon as you can. These items may include a multi-tool or Swiss Army knife, large belt knife, N95 respirators, canteen (filled) with belt hanger, handgun or pepper spray, ammunition magazines, small flashlight, sunglasses, cap, gloves, fire starter or waterproof matches, evacuation route maps, personal medications, spare eyeglasses, compass, and small first aid kit. I carry a Smith and Wesson brand KA-BAR-style knife with a six-inch blade or an Air Force survival knife with a five-inch blade and a fourteen-function multi-tool with its pliers, saws, files, screwdrivers, and blades.

About This Pack

The pack described below is a compromise based on what the *average* person can afford and carry. It is intended to provide all the basic needs for one person for three to five days and provide considerable support beyond that time. You would need to seek improved shelter and food sources as soon as possible. Foraging, fishing, and hunting skills would be needed to extend independent survival. Carrying a tent and sleeping bag adds more weight than most evacuees can carry, so the shelter and warmth components are minimized to save weight. However, this limits the range of weather conditions in which you can expect to be comfortable. The use of foraged natural and man-made materials would be required in severe weather.

This pack should keep you comfortable in warm, dry weather; be adequate in cool and damp weather; and help you survive in cold (below 40 degrees) weather. In conditions of severe cold and wind, the BTN rule applies. It may be advisable to reconfigure the pack in late fall with more weight for warmth and less weight for other items. I have redundant systems for shelter, fire, food, and water purification because these are the most essential needs.

There are acceptable substitutes for every item depending on preferences and budget. Some items can be bought off-the-shelf or made at home. You may choose to replace some items with very high-end products or cheap BTN substitutes. You may want to put together a "starter pack" that covers each need with some items and then upgrade to better products as soon as possible. Remember that a fair survival pack you have ready is going to do you a lot more good than a great survival pack you are planning. Survival is 50 percent what you can do and 50 percent what you can do without. So think about each item you put into the pack and how you will use it. You want to breathe clean air, drink uncontaminated water, eat safe food, stay warm and dry, remain healthy, and protect yourself. That's it! Everything else is secondary.

1. AIR

In many survival situations, you may need to improve the air you are breathing. The air may be filled with dust, smoke, and toxic material as you escape a disaster area. It may be very cold, so breathing through a mask may help prewarm the air and reduce your heat loss. There may be biological organisms in a populated area that carry deadly diseases. For all the above hazards, I have several N95 and N99 soft respirators in the outer pack pockets. N95 masks are rated as 95-percent effective at filtering three-micron particulates but are proven effective at much smaller sizes. The chances of encountering a chemical agent (poison gas) situation are very small, so for most of us the bulk and weight of a military or civilian chemical mask are unnecessary. However, if you are concerned about such a threat, you may want to have one of the masks sold for use in spraying pesticides and a pair of the closed goggles that are available in most home improvement stores. But when properly fitted, the N95 and N99 are adequate, as well as cheap, light, and small.

2. WATER

The most common and essential survival need is water, so redundant sources should be available. Include a quart-filled water bottle for immediate use, a water-purification filter system that will purify one thousand gallons of water, and water purification tablets that will purify twenty-five additional quarts. All are available at any sporting goods stores. Water purification is covered in more detail in Chapter 9.

Left to right: Water purification tablets, water-filtration straw, water-filtration canteen, and portable water-filtration system for campers.

3. SHELTER AND WARMTH

Most tents are just too heavy, and the weight and space drastically reduce food capacity. I carry a one-millimeter-thick 10x20-foot tarp (drop cloth), which is big enough to provide full shelter in most conditions. It may not last more than a few days under some conditions, but it is light. Then I have a good-quality military rain poncho that can be worn in bad weather or used for a shelter or ground cloth. I have the military poncho liner to go with it as a blanket. You can get equivalent ponchos and light blankets or bags at sporting good and surplus stores. Finally, I have included a high-quality space blanket with its quilted and reflective surface. I have slept out in a plastic shelter with an army blanket and a space blanket at below zero wind-chills. Yes, it was cold. I slept on and off with all my clothes on, but I survived. This is survival, not a stay at the Ritz.

Lock picks or a lock pick gun may be worth the weight. In a large-scale disaster, plenty of abandoned commercial, industrial, and residential structures will be empty. (See Chapter 12, "Ten Shelters You Should Know How to Build.")

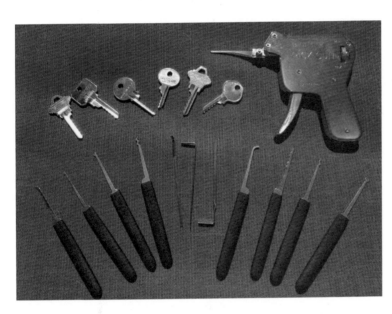

Bump keys (top left), lock pick guns (top right), or a set of lock picks (bottom) can provide access to shelter in desperate situations. You do need to practice with them before you need them.

4. FOOD AND FOOD PREPARATION

Most Americans are accustomed to eating whenever they want (whether or not they are hungry) and often eat a lot more than the recommended 2,000 calories per day. In theory, you can live several weeks without any food at all, but endurance and judgment can begin to deteriorate after a few days without nourishment. You can go a long way on survival rations of much less than 2,000 calories per day. Carrying and consuming 2,000-calorie meals for three to five days would take up unacceptable weight and space. My food choices are based on what would keep me going for long enough to establish other food sources. Obviously, any additional food I could forage or hunt would extend my rations.

I have also included a slingshot, snare wire, and a fishing kit with hooks, line, sinkers, and other items to help gather food. The miniature survival book illustrates ways to catch fish and game, and how to identify some edible plants. I also have a slingshot and a survival bow for taking game silently and a modified .22-caliber AR-7 survival rifle and ammunition. All three together weigh only a few pounds and take up little room.

I have found that carrying a miniature stove, fuel cans, and dehydrated meals is more effective than carrying self-heating meals for fast hot food. I carry four freeze-dried camp meals. I also carry a package of eighteen Lifeboat Ration Bars that are two hundred calories each. They are not all that tasty, but they will keep you going. Some coffee or tea bags and sugar add little weight and provide much comfort. Lastly, I throw some trail snacks and energy bars in with the pack to go in the pockets. To prepare food I have a standard camping mess kit and a miniature stove and two fuel cartridges. You may substitute a folding Nesbit stove with fuel tablets that burn nine minutes each. This is just in case I cannot make a campfire. Of course, I also have a knife, fork, and spoon set.

You may want to save money by packing such foods as rice, pasta, beans, cornmeal, oatmeal, dried fruits, nuts, and jerky. That's what they did in the old days. Even packages of instant oatmeal, macaroni and cheese, and Rice-A-Roni can work. It takes more time and energy to fix these and they are a bit bulkier and heavier, but they provide an alternative. These foods do need to be rotated and replaced at least annually, since they don't keep as well as freeze-dried rations. (See Chapter 10 for other alternatives.)

A few samples of packable survival foods. Some require more frequent rotation than others. Note the bouillon cubes at left; beef and chicken bouillon cubes and various seasonings can make foraged foods more palatable.

Left to right: Coghlan's folding stove that uses canned alcohol, miniature butane stove, and fold-flat stove that uses heat tablets. Store medications and personal hygiene items in plastic bags.

5. HEAT AND LIGHT SOURCES

This is another area where you want redundancy. You want to have a good-quality, medium-sized, solar-chargeable LED flashlight. Add a couple of chemical light sticks and a few of the small tea candles that burn for up to four hours and you have reliable light. For fire-starting, I have several packs of waterproof matches, a butane lighter, and the last resort: a magnesium fire striker. I have also found that a cheap welding striker with extra flints is a very reliable fire starter. (More details about fires are covered in Chapter 11, "Ten Ways to Start and Maintain a Fire.")

6. SANITATION AND PERSONAL HYGIENE

A small bottle of liquid soap, a washcloth, and a small towel will permit hand and face washing and even sponge baths as needed. A travel-size toothbrush and toothpaste, razor, and an unbreakable camp mirror complete the kit. A bottle of good insect repellent is highly recommended. There may be a few other items to suit your personal needs. *Note:* Be sure to dry the washcloth and towel thoroughly before placing in the pack. Damp items will quickly breed mold.

7. FIRST AID AND HEALTH

The size and contents of your first aid kit will depend on your medical condition, your anticipated injuries (e.g., gun shots, fractures, snakebite), and your level of medical skills. A small first aid manual is a good addition to the kit if space permits. Be sure to include a package of blood stopper or a quick-clot gauze pad. This stuff will stop even heavy arterial bleeding.

Including a tourniquet device may be a good idea too. The first aid kit should include several 3x3-inch gauze pads, an assortment of Band-Aids, a 2-inch-wide elastic bandage, a pair of latex gloves, a CPR mask, small tubes of Neosporin and hydrocortisone, about six antiseptic wipes, packages of Tylenol, Advil,* aspirin, antacids, and a small bottle of eye wash. A good pair of tweezers, a pair of single blunt medical scissors, and a small hemostat should also be included. If you have dentures, include a denture repair kit. If not, then be sure to include a dental first aid kit.

Don't forget to include any prescription or over-the-counter medications you require for your individual health conditions. Remember that the pharmacies will likely be closed or looted. Finally, have a spare pair of eyeglasses or a small magnifying glass in a well-padded location. You will need to do a lot of careful work and read the small print on your maps and survival instructions. That roll of electrical tape carried in the repair supplies can also be used for holding bandages, so I do not add a roll of medical tape to the kit.

* Three Advil and two Tylenol tablets can be taken safely together and will provide many times the pain relief of the same taken separately. This is for severe pain where prescription pain relievers are unavailable.

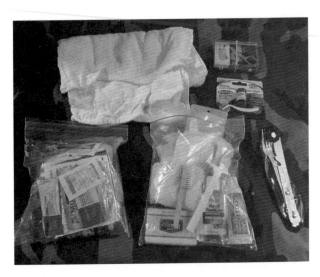

Store-bought first aid kit and first aid manual, with compact tourniquet in center.

8. INFORMATION AND PLANS

All family members should know the emergency plans by heart, but key information should be kept in the pack so that details are not forgotten over time. Remember that some or all of the family members may be away from home when the situation develops. Your plans should include the following:

- One or more alternative rendezvous points if you cannot get home or must leave home before others can return.
- Alternative shelter-in-place locations if you cannot get home or to the rendezvous point quickly.
- Clearly understood what-if action plans for every likely emergency (e.g., home fire, civil disorder, intruder, epidemic, evacuation) and what family or group member does what, when, and how. (See Chapter 2 for detailed disaster action plans.)
- Have coded communications, such as, "If I say the code word you all know to follow the plan" or "In an emergency, leave a message at or with . . ." Don't be totally dependent on cell phones or landlines.
- Have copies of all your critical documents, including birth certificates, medical records, marriage licenses, vehicle titles, mortgage papers, bank accounts, and insurance policies. You may want to transfer these to a very secure location on your person to assure that they are not stolen or lost.
- A small pair of binoculars is a must. Anything that lets you see the route ahead will save you time and energy. Anything that lets you see who is coming or who is at the place you are going before he sees you could save your life.
- Have a small AM/FM/weather band radio. Select one that has solar- and crank-power capabilities. Many now can also recharge your cell phone. Even though you may need to be on your own, it is important to know the weather and what threats are developing and where.
- Even experienced survivalists don't remember everything they need to know, so include a miniature survival guide book or survival cards that contains loads of information on first aid, foraging, trapping, fishing, and building shelters.
- You should have a good topographical map of the area within a few hundred miles of your home and any area to which you may be going. The best maps are the ones in the state atlases and gazetteers available at truck stops because they show most of the side roads as well.

9. CLOTHING

A good-quality rain poncho is an absolute must since keeping dry is essential. I don't have room for a change of clothing, but I have included a wool cap because the body loses most of its heat through the top of the head. The pioneers used to say that if your feet are cold, put on your hat. They were right. But just in case, I have two extra pairs of socks as well. I also managed to stuff in one Tyvek chemical suit. This does not weigh much and can be used for an NBC-protection

Top row: Military rain poncho, space blanket, warm socks. Bottom row: Parachute cord for rigging shelter, N95 dust mask, compact rescue blanket (for small kits), stocking cap.

outer garment or an alternative garment to wear while drying or cleaning your main clothing. You may want to consider keeping a full set of winter clothing in a separate bag with your pack.

10. WEAPONS

Since you may truly have to "grab and go," you should have at least one firearm in or next to your pack. The selection of weapons for a survival pack is the subject of endless controversy. Some may want to go without a firearm. Okay, carry a good-sized can of pepper spray and hope for the best, but this is survival and less responsible (using kind words here) citizens may be quite prepared to take what you have by force. Depending on your environment, you have two options for carrying a firearm under survival conditions. If you are going to be evacuating through reasonably civilized areas, you may want to go for a concealed carry (with or without permit) with a small handgun inside the pack or in a pocket. A small .22-caliber handgun in the pack with a few hundred rounds will give you lots of small-game hunting potential and some deterrent to would-be attackers. A .380 or small 9mm automatic in the pocket gives you a little more power, but is still easy to conceal. If law and order has broken down or you are moving directly into a rural or wilderness environment, you may as well

Three weapons primarily for hunting: (far left) survival slingshot, (top center) AR-7 .22-caliber survival rifle with its bulky floating stock replaced with compact folding stock, (bottom center and right) survival bow disassembled. The bow and the arrows fit in the pouch on the right and assemble in about a minute. All three weapons take up very little room in the pack.

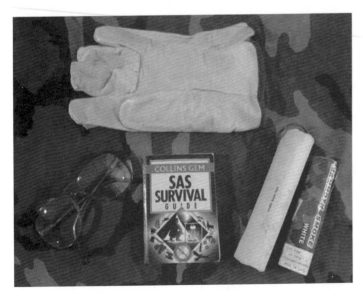

Gloves are an important addition to any survival pack, as are extra glasses. Unless you have a photographic memory, a small survival manual may come in handy. The smoke bombs at right can be used to cover your movement, create distractions, and signal for help.

carry a full-size 9mm or .40-caliber handgun on your belt or a rifle or shotgun in your hand. Since these larger weapons do not go *in* the pack, they are covered elsewhere as home-defense weapons.

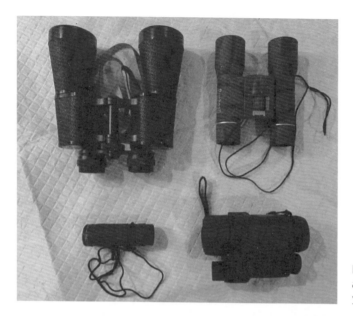

Binoculars come in a variety of sizes, powers, and qualities. If weight and space are limited, you can even get by with a small monocular.

Dig in, dig up, dig out, or bury. A small shovel is a necessity in survival situations.

Miscellaneous Must-Haves

You should have a good-quality compass, but it will not be of much value unless you take the time to learn how to use it. I have a small sewing kit with needles, thread, safety pins, and scissors for clothing repairs. The needles, pins, and scissors are also handy for some first aid procedures. I also include fifty feet of nylon parachute cord for shelter building, animal trapping, and other emergencies. I have a very small folding shovel attached to the pack. This is required for sanitation, clearing ground for a camp, and digging a shelter if necessary. You may want to save money and weight by just carrying a good garden trowel. A whistle is a must for those cases where you do need to attract attention. A role of electrical tape is great for making all sorts of repairs.

I also carry two or three smoke bombs. These can be thrown out to screen an area you must cross or a person who must be rescued. Smoke bombs burn only a few minutes, and you must carefully consider the wind direction, wind velocity, and timing. A wind shift that puts you in front of the smoke can silhouette you for a shooter. How many smoke bombs you have will depend on what kinds of situations you anticipate and what areas you may need to get through. I have found that yellow and orange smoke is the most effective for screening as well as for getting attention. You can get fused multi-colored smoke bombs at fireworks stores for about $2.50 each. These are fairly effective, but the paintball business has resulted in a variety of better smoke "grenades" in all colors that are ignited by pulling a ring. I found smoke grenades ranging from 25,000 cubic feet of smoke for $8.95 each to 70,000 cubic feet for $17.95.

Surviving with Your Pack (A Scenario)

February 18, 2018. It has been twelve days since the first signs of the epidemic were recognized. You wisely stocked up on a few items you did not already have before the panic started. You also filled up every container you could find with water and fueled your vehicles. Eight days ago, the hospitals started to get swamped, and the stores had sold out of food, bottled water, medical supplies, flashlights, firearms, and generators. All the shoppers in those stores only accelerated the spread of the unknown virus.

Government agencies are not sure whether the source is a terrorist attack or some new mutated flu virus. They have called out the National Guard and requested that all nonessential persons stay at home. You have been able to stay in your house because you had enough food supplies, but three days ago the electric power went off because the power company employees stayed home or were sick. Police, fire, and emergency medical services are no longer functioning, and criminal attacks and looting are breaking out in your community.

You can see smoke from uncontrolled fires a few blocks away, and you hear shooting. You have been using some of the items from your survival pack already, but you have kept it packed and ready. Today the water stopped running, and a fire is spreading down your street. You throw your pack and a few other items in your vehicle and try to drive out to a safer area, but, after a few miles, disabled vehicles and gang activities block the roads. You abandon your vehicle and take your pack and a rifle down alleys until you reach an abandoned railroad right-of-way that is on your map.

You spend the first night in an abandoned building, where you drink from your canteen and eat one of your heater meals. You then wrap up in your space blanket and get some sleep. Eating an energy bar, you continue your evacuation. You wear your mask and clean your hands frequently to avoid contamination from others who may have been in the same locations. Once, several teenage gang members who wanted your pack confronted you, but a few warning shots were enough to send them running this time.

You use your binoculars to avoid hazards and find safe routes ahead. You have walked far enough to get out of the suburbs, into a semirural area where there are some wooded areas. You selected a well-concealed location and set up a camp. The plastic tarp seals your improvised shelter, and you are able to use your stove or build a small fire to cook your food.* You filter water gathered from a nearby creek through your water purification system, and you are reasonably warm with your survival blanket and insulated liner. You listen to your small radio and find out that the epidemic is slowly diminishing. Hundreds of thousands have died of the disease, rioting, and starvation. Most of those who were able to stay isolated for thirty days or more were able to avoid the contamination and violence. You elect to stay in the woods for another ten days, using your pack equipment to hunt and fish.

Of course, this is a worst-case scenario and does not involve the more complex issues of a family, but try running this or any other serious disaster scenario without that survival pack. You would be out there hungry, freezing, thirsty, getting contaminated, fighting, getting injured, being desperate, and having a lot fewer options.

Suggested Seventy-Two-Hour Emergency Backpack

The list below is a slightly modified version of the FEMA seventy-two-hour evacuation pack. It is lighter than a true survival pack but is only intended to get you through a few hours until you reach help or help reaches you. It's a good starting point but may prove inadequate under long-term and severe emergencies. Note that it does not include any kind of weapon. A true survival knife and a large can of pepper spray would be the minimum advisable self-defense weapons even for these limited situations. Certainly a handgun and extra ammunition should be considered for urban evacuations, but be aware that government aid agencies may want to confiscate these at roadblocks or at shelters.

- (4) Sixteen-ounce water bottles
- (1) Collapsible stove with heat tablets*
- (1) Metal canteen cup or Sierra cup
- (1) Fifty-hour candle (optional ten tea candles)
- (1) Five LED flashlight
- (1) Multi-band radio (AM/FM/weather; crank/solar/battery powered)
- Food bars (3,000 to 4,000 calories each)
- (1) Large rain poncho
- (2) N95 dust/mist respirators
- (1) Space blanket (alternate: tube tent)
- (1) Multi-function knife
- (1) Box waterproof matches
- (1) Bottle of water purification tablets (or filter device)
- (1) Bottle of hand sanitizer
- (1) First aid kit
- . (1) Pair extra glasses
- (1) Spare pair of heavy socks
- Extra prescription medications
- (6) Light sticks
- Copies of birth certificates, deeds, mortgages, titles, insurance papers, and medical and contact information.

* These can be used to warm a vehicle or shelter, or to boil water or heat optional packets of coffee, tea, or hot chocolate in cold weather.

Note: Keep good hiking shoes with your pack. You do not want to flee into the street or woods in flip-flops or slippers.

CHAPTER 6
Ten Ways to Avoid and Survive Street Crime

I am probably one of the few "survivalist" writers who has actually lived in a high-crime urban environment for an extended period. In fact, I resided and worked in the Pullman-Roseland section of Chicago's far Southside for most of my life, where graffiti, gunshots, and groups of hooded teens were normal. While you could go about your daily business most of the time without too much trouble, it was essential to maintain a lifestyle and alert level much different than what rural or suburban residents would maintain. Being a student of military strategy, I tended to apply strategic and tactical principles to my street survival methods.

You Versus the Enemy

Criminals are basically dumb and cowardly—that's why they are criminals. To offset this lack of intelligence, they have developed instincts and what is known as "street smarts." The great majority of intelligent, working, and responsible people do not have well-developed street instincts and have not had the years of developing street smarts that the criminals have, so they are at a great disadvantage in a street crime situation. In many ways, the citizen is in the same situation as a conventional army confronted by a guerrilla ambush. You are carrying out normal operations and are deployed and equipped for getting to work or buying groceries, whereas the criminal has the initiative in selecting the time, place, and method of attack. He will want to strike hard and fast, and get away without being pressed or pinned down. The average street crime takes from four to six seconds from the time the victim realizes it's happening till the time the criminal is gone. In the streets of today's urban areas, a little paranoia is just very good thinking. Whether you're walking or driving in your car, you should be thinking a little like you are on a combat patrol where you are the point man, the squad leader, and the rear guard.

1. AVOID BEING A VICTIM

Deny the enemy a tempting target. Plan your route to avoid high-crime areas, empty parking lots, dark alleys, and other risky spots, and if you must move through such areas, plan to do it at times when it is light and most crowded. As much as possible, avoid being on the criminal's ground (e.g., alleys, dark streets, bad neighborhoods). If he aims to commit a crime against you, let him come to you on ground that *you* know well.

Deny the enemy confidence. One thing a criminal does not want is a fight, so he looks for "soft" targets. A person walking along daydreaming, talking or texting on a cell phone, or looking down at the pavement tells the attacker that this target is not alert and is probably submissive. If you are marching along with purpose, scanning the area for threats, and holding your head high, the criminal will probably look for someone else to attack. Clothing can help to discourage attackers. Someone wearing boots, a leather jacket, and a buck knife on his belt is a lot less likely to get jumped than someone wearing sandals, shorts, and a sweater. If you encounter a person (or persons) coming toward you, never (*I mean never*) look down—keep your head up and look past him. Remember downcast eyes say, "I am submissive and will do what you tell me to do." Never let a criminal or anyone think that! Remember, all the criminal knows about you is what he sees. So if you look like trouble, he has to assume you could *be* trouble, which is the last thing he wants.

2. ARMED ROBBERY ON THE STREET

Be especially vigilant leaving banks, ATMs, restaurants, and other locations where criminals may be waiting for victims. Walk fast and do not stop moving. If approached by a panhandler or someone asking directions, keep moving and avoid any doorways or dead ends. Move the stranger where you want to go, not where he wants you to go. Criminals often work in pairs. One is going to stop you while the other comes up behind or out of hiding nearby. Pickpockets and purse thieves work this way too. One innocent-seeming person stops you for directions or to ask a question while the other lifts your wallet, cell phone, or purse. This happens in grocery stores and parking lots regularly.

Rest assured that the criminal or gangbanger has a plan. His plan will be simple because he is simple. You must have a plan too, and your plan must be simple because you are smart and know that simple plans work. Remember, you only have four to six seconds, so you must know exactly what you are going to do and have confidence that it will work because you have practiced and can react immediately. Your plan might be "I will scream and kick like hell," or "I will throw my bag and run the other way," or "I will start yelling fire as loud as I can." One possibility is to have a money clip with a few dollars in it (the clip gives it weight) that you can throw in one direction while running in the other direction. Consider routes of escape and potential safe havens to head for, such as open stores, well-lit areas, or gas stations. Inventory your weapons (everything you have can be a weapon) and ways in which they can be used. Your immediate action will disrupt the criminal's plan and put you in control.

3. WALKING INTO A CRIME

Anywhere there is money or salable goods is a target for armed robbers. Store employees and customers are often robbed and beaten as well. Criminals usually try to hit such locations when there are fewer customers, but accidently walking in on such a situation can have tragic consequences. Police officers never approach a store or other facility straight from the front. They will park off to the side and approach from the side and glance into the window or door before walking in. Spotting suspicious people in the store, damaged locks, an empty counter, or an occupied running vehicle (e.g., get-away driver, lookout) is a sign that a crime may be in progress. Gas stations, banks, sandwich shops, hair salons, and smoke shops are frequent targets. Closing time makes any business extra vulnerable. Walking in on such a situation could result in your being robbed, at best, or being killed, worst case. Being alert for signs of a crime in progress, retreating to a safe distance, and calling 911 if your suspicions are substantiated is a better option than blundering into trouble.

4. DRIVE-BY SHOOTING

A drive-by shooting is almost always a deliberate act by gang members in urban areas. Your best defense is to avoid being associated with gangs and gang members and frequenting gang-infested areas. Be aware that gang-retaliation shootings frequently target innocent friends and relatives of gang members. Even children are often targeted. Know your associates and contacts. In some areas it's not the bullet with your name on it that you need to worry about. It's the bullet addressed "to whom it may concern." At the first sign of weapons being deployed, find cover (see Principle 7, "Active Shooter," in this chapter), but if that's not immediately available, just get down and lie flat until the shooting has stopped and the shooters' vehicles have left. Then get to better cover in case they return. Drive-by shootings are highly inaccurate and there is no safe zone away from the targets. *Get down right away!* If you are in a building and hear gunshots, bullets may come through windows or right through the walls, so do the following:

- Do not go to the window.
- Do not go outside.
- Do lie down flat on the floor and stay there.
- Do turn out lights if there is time and opportunity.

The convex mirror gives a better view of the vehicle's close side.

5. CARJACKING

Park your vehicle in a well-lit area. When coming out of a building, look around for suspicious people loitering nearby before approaching your car. If concerned, go back inside and get others to accompany you. Do not go directly toward your vehicle or activate the unlock button until you are ready to jump in. This keeps potential assailants from intercepting you. Try to observe under and around your vehicle and adjoining ones as you approach. Windowless vans with sliding doors close to your driver's side are particularly suspicious. Lock your door immediately upon entry, and always drive with your doors locked! Do not, under any circumstances, stop for someone other than a police officer flagging you down on the street. This is a common technique is used by criminals to make Good Samaritans into victims.

Be vigilant at stop lights, especially at uninhabited intersections. If someone points a gun at you while you are stopped, you have three options:

1. Drive through the intersection.
2. Say okay to his demands, slide out the passenger side, and run, leaving the carjacker with the running car.
3. Turn off the vehicle, get out, and throw the keys one way while running the other.

Whichever you do, do it fast. Never let the criminal get into the vehicle with you still inside or make you get back into the vehicle.

Carjackers and snatch-and-run thieves will approach from your blind spot while you sit at a traffic light or in a parking lot. Adding a convex mirror to your side mirrors can help you spot them as they approach close to the side of your vehicle. A mirror or two in your trunk lid will help you spot attackers who close in on you while you are loading or unloading groceries.

6. ABDUCTION

Usually the abductor will say something like "Do as I say and you won't get hurt." This is always a lie. Just like the guerrilla ambush, the criminal does not want to have the cavalry show up and pin him down, so stay where there are other people, good lighting, and high visibility. Abductors will take your cell phone immediately but will seldom look for a second one. Having an old non-connected one to give them leaves you with a traceable one to help the police find you. Set it on silent mode so it will not be detected if someone calls you.

Never get into a car with a criminal! If a criminal points a gun at you and says, "Get in the car," run like hell. The chance that he will shoot at you is about fifty-fifty; the chance that he will hit you if he does shoot is about fifty-fifty; the chances that the wound will be fatal if he does manage to hit you is less than fifty-fifty. So your chance of survival if you run is about 90 percent! On the other hand, crime statistics show that your chances of being found dead if you get into a car with a criminal are almost 100 percent. *Don't get in the car!*

If you are abducted, your chances of escape and survival decline with every minute you do not act. The criminal has to disable you and get you to his primary crime scene location to do bad things. Do everything in your power to get away and draw attention before that happens. If you are put into a trunk, most newer vehicles have trunk releases inside. You can also kick out the taillight from inside to get attention. Do not hesitate to cause the vehicle to crash in a populated area or jump out of a moving vehicle. Your chances of surviving such a move are far better than letting him take you to a secluded location of his choice. Be alert for potential tools and weapons in vehicles and wherever he takes you.

Carrying the items recommended in Chapter 4, "Ten Items You Should Always Carry," will give you a great advantage in these situations.

7. ACTIVE SHOOTER

Active-shooter situations are becoming more frequent in our country. An active shooter is someone who initiates a shooting and then continues to shoot multiple rounds at multiple victims. Active shooters target crowded locations, such as malls, theaters, clubs, and public buildings, where every round fired may hit one or more victims. If caught in this situation, you can be sure that the killing will continue until either the police engage the shooter or the shooter has killed everyone within sight. Even the police have now admitted that civilians caught in such situations should take certain actions rather than stay calm or try to reason with the terrorists.

Unfortunately, the days when you could relax and enjoy public places and public venues are gone. Violent assaults, gang wars, drive-by shootings, and terrorist guns and bombs have converted our communities into potential war zones. Below are steps and actions that give you the best chance to survive such an event.

Being Prepared for a Potential Active Shooter Situation

- **Be observant and alert**. In any crowd, you must observe for suspicious behavior. Are people wearing unnecessarily baggy or long clothing? Do some have suspicious bulges in their clothing, or are they carrying odd, long packages? Are some wearing backpacks or abandoning backpacks? Are some moving around suspiciously and looking around as if getting ready to take some action? If your "sixth sense" is telling you to get out or get down, then do it!
- **Make an escape plan**. In a restaurant, mall, theater, or other potential terrorist target, you should constantly be aware of where the exits are. Exits can be fire doors, windows, railings, or anything that works. Consider routes to all exits that offer the most bulletproof cover. If true escape is not safe, then seek any room with a solid door that can be locked and barricaded with heavy furniture.
- **Identify potential bulletproof cover**. While you may hide behind furniture, car bodies, and plaster or wood walls, they generally will not stop bullets. They provide only concealment. Bulletproof cover is offered by brick or concrete walls, cement walls, heavy appliances, engine blocks, and other very solid objects. Constantly identify these as places to go to if escape is not immediately available.

What to Do When the First Shots are Fired

- **Act immediately**. If you have accepted the possibility of an active-shooter situation and taken the steps above, you can skip from denial to action while others freeze and get shot.

- **Take cover**. If you are already in the shooter's vision or if there is no covered escape route that will not expose you to the shooter, taking cover may be your only option. Immediately get behind the strongest, thickest object possible. Stay low or lie flat. If you are wounded or among wounded people, lie down and play dead. Shooters will instinctively shoot at anyone they see moving.

- **Escape**. If the shooter has his back to you, you have a chance to escape or at least reach good cover before he turns around. But remember that there may be more than one shooter. If you go through a door, get to the right or left of the door and keep moving toward cover since the shooter may shoot through it or follow you out.

- **Engage**. The Washington, DC, chief of police and many others have now recognized that civilians may need to take action on their own before law enforcement arrives to save themselves and others. If you cannot escape or find cover and the shooter continues to shoot, your best chance is to distract, delay, or disable the shooter. Discharging a fire extinguisher; throwing a heavy object; and tackling, clubbing, or stabbing the shooter are all justified in this situation. If you have a firearm, use it. Yes, shoot the shooter in the back if you can. Aim for the head as active shooters often wear bulletproof vests. If possible, shoot from a low position so your bullets go upward and avoid hitting bystanders. Don't hesitate and don't try to get a shooter to surrender; he will just shoot you. Caution: Remember, the police will consider anyone they find holding a gun as the enemy. Once the shooter is down, you can kick his weapon(s) out of his reach but do not pick it up. Then put your weapon down and your hands up, and wait for the police.

- **Communicate**. If not in immediate danger, use your cell phone to call for help. Provide the police with any information that you can, such as the description and number of shooters, location of shooters, type of weapons used, and the direction shooters are moving or did move. If you are barricaded or behind cover, provide your location and your own description. If nothing else, pull the fire alarm to warn others and distract the shooter.

- **Recovery**. If you are lucky enough to initially survive a mass shooting, you are not safe yet because the police are going to be very jumpy on entry. Stay down and keep your hands up. Follow police instructions carefully. Officers will consider everyone there as a threat until they are searched, interviewed, and cleared. There may still be other active shooters at large or there may be bombs or booby traps left behind. If you are carrying a firearm (open or concealed), be sure to immediately tell the police while keeping your hands up. If you have any medical training, try to help the wounded until the medics arrive. Stopping severe bleeding and treating for shock may save lives.

8. ELEVATORS AND TRAINS

Elevators and train cars are frequently the scene of crimes. Distracted passengers often step into such vehicles without even looking. Once inside, they are trapped with the assailants. Sadly, even if there are witnesses, they may choose not to help or get involved. Thieves may snatch your purse or wallet just as you board a train or get on an elevator, or pick your pocket while in these conveyances. Armed robberies, beatings, and rapes have occurred on elevators and commuter trains. Try to sit near the exit door or the door to adjoining cars to have an escape route.

If you are about to board an elevator or a commuter car and don't like the looks of someone onboard, don't get in. It is far better to ride the next elevator or train than the next ambulance. Listen to your instincts! If you are in the elevator and someone gets on who arouses your suspicion, get off immediately. If suspicious or disruptive individuals board your commuter car, get off and wait for the next train, move to another car quickly, or pull the emergency cord. Have a plan.

If attacked in the elevator, *do not push the emergency button!* This will stop the elevator. Instead push all the floor buttons and try to prevent the attacker from pushing the emergency button. This way you have an escape opportunity every few seconds when the door opens at each floor.

9. APPROACHING A POTENTIAL THREAT

It was pretty hard to avoid "potential" threats while walking around in south Chicago. I practiced the habits described above to avoid looking like a victim. I also changed my routes regularly and completely avoided ones that I considered especially hazardous. Sometimes potential trouble turned out to be innocent, but it's always better to be ready. When a potential assailant (probably not) was coming toward me on a lonely street, I tended to unzip my jacket and position my hands higher. Someone with bad intentions would think I might have a gun. I always passed doorways and blind corners wide and out toward the street. This gave me some time and space to react if trouble was indeed hiding there. If I observed multiple suspicious persons gathered on or near my route, I had no hesitation about turning in another direction. Most important, I always looked around and regularly checked my six o'clock position. In passing anyone, I never looked down but never made eye contact. I looked just behind the individual, alert for anything.

Sometimes you just have to punt. I came around a corner walking fast and found six drug dealers gathered directly in my path, four feet in front of me. It was too late to turn around and unwise to stop. I cut between them, said, "Excuse me, guys," and kept going. Surprise and speed were all I had.

10. CHILD PROTECTION

Being raised in a poor, high-crime area myself and aiding children in "the projects" to avoid the worst of their environment provided much of what follows. Other material is drawn from law enforcement and child safety sources.

Today's children are at risk from a variety of threats, yet our society discourages even basic self-protection and resistance. So-called zero tolerance policies punish victims and offenders alike, and prohibit any kind of active defense. "Helicopter parents" try to monitor and manage their children round-the-clock to protect them from every conceivable source of stress and hazard.

Being overly protective and over restrictive of children usually results in rebellion and resistance. Overprotected children may become dependent, insecure, and unable to survive in the real world. The best thing you can do for the safety of your children is to teach them to survive when you're not there.

Teach children that most people are good and kind, but be sure they understand that there are some very bad people out there too. Have conversations with them about personal safety and street survival. When events involving children (accidents or crimes) are in the news, talk to them about it. Discuss the actions, consequences, and precautions involved.

Rid the kids of bad habits, such as wearing headphones or focusing on a smart phone while on the streets. This makes them a sitting duck for criminals of all kinds, not to mention accidents. Teach them to be aware of their surroundings and people. Are you being watched? Are you being followed? Are those gang members on the corner?

Teach them the following habits and survival actions:

- Try to walk and bike with friends, never alone.
- Never get into a vehicle with anyone you do not know well, even if the individual claims to know your parents or friends.
- Never fall for the offer of a ride, candy, or other temptation.
- Never go anywhere with anyone you don't know well.
- Even if threatened with a weapon in a public area, do not go with a stranger or keep quiet. Run and scream immediately. Many children have gone quietly with abductors from busy streets and shopping malls to be molested and killed at a remote location.
- If approached by a stranger, keep your distance and tell the person to stop coming before he can get close enough to grab you. Avoid getting caught in a place from which you can't escape. If the person keeps coming, run and scream. If he grabs you, kick, bite, scratch, kick the crotch, and poke the eyes.

While today's children are prohibited from having any sort of defense device in school, they certainly can have a whistle to call for help. Children should be taught basic self-protection and escape (from holds) moves, and attend self-defense classes. Teach the child the best actions to take if caught in an active-shooter or drive-by shooting incident. Basically: get down, get out, or get behind cover. They should understand how horrible getting shot is. (See "Drive-by Shooting" and "Active Shooter" sections of this chapter.)

Raising Survivors

Sexual predators, drug peddlers, and gang recruiters look for children who lack self-confidence and self-esteem. Such children are drawn to sources of inclusion, comfort, security, membership, and leadership. To vaccinate children against such people, you must make them survivors.

- The family (even if small) must become a valuable haven and an example for life.
- Be aware of your children and what they are thinking and doing. They are not really entitled to privacy or secrecy. Talk with them. Ask questions. Be alert for changes in behavior. Care and share.
- Reinforce the child's sense of self-worth and value to the family and the community.
- Set examples of good moral conduct, safety, and responsibility.
- Participate in your local community and schools.
- Establish firm but reasonable rules. Don't be afraid to enforce rules in a reasonable way.
- Most children always want to fit in. Be sure they have the right things to fit in to. Don't be afraid to intervene if their associations are unhealthy. Only fools fit in with fools.
- Always remember that you are a parent first and a buddy second.
- As the child matures, be sure that he or she has hopes, dreams, and plans for the future. Adolescents tend to think that now is everything, so when now looks bad they make big errors or even commit suicide. Make them aware of a hopeful future and things to look forward to.

If Your Child Goes Missing

Missing children are everyone's worst nightmare. As children in the late 1940s, we were told to have fun and "come home before the streetlights come on." That could be as long as eight to ten hours without parental contact or supervision. Today an absence or failure to check in of more than a few hours may generate panic.

The police are not going to throw a lot of resources into a missing child unless it has been over twenty-four hours or there are other factors, such as inclement weather, disability, custody issues, or threats of violence or evidence of violence or abduction. Ninety-nine percent of missing children turn up within one to two days. After that, the chances of recovery become much less. Children over the age of consent cannot be forced to return even if found by police. If you are sure something is wrong, report it to the police and then start checking with the child's friends and places where he or she might hang out or be in danger. If you can't locate the child within a day or find information indicating foul play, get back to the police immediately.

No matter what the situation, loved, confident, self-reliant children are much less likely to do drugs, join gangs, run away, or commit suicide. They are survivors in emergencies and successful in life.

Addendum: How to Avoid Children Being Shot by the Police

The police do not just go around shooting innocent people walking down the street. Although some police shootings turn out to be overreactions or accidents, most were in situations precipitated by the victim's criminal activities or failure to promptly obey police commands. If a person appears to be armed or a threat to others, or fails to obey commands, the police are justified to use deadly force. They are not allowed to simply let the offender run off. To not do everything in their power to detain the suspect is called "failure of duty," and the officer or officers are subject to disciplinary action and possible termination. They are not obligated to try to chase and tackle an offender who may well be faster and stronger than they are. They are obliged to stop the offender by the most effective means necessary while minimizing the risk of injury to themselves and others. Actually the way to avoid being shot is pretty simple.

Young Adults and Teenagers

- Don't be involved in criminal activities.
- Don't do drugs.
- Don't hang around gangs or act and dress like a gang member.

- Don't run when the police say stop.
- Don't point things (anything) at the police.
- Stop and obey every police order immediately.
- Do not fight or struggle with officers.

Parents: How to Prevent Your Children from Being Shot by the Police

- Do not tolerate and enable your children's participation in any kind of criminal, gang-, or drug-related activities.
- Do not tolerate criminal activities or drug usage by friends and family.
- Teach children the above rules for avoiding violent police–civilian confrontations.
- Teach them self-respect, respect for others, and respect for the law.
- Make them safe, responsible, and productive citizens.

CHAPTER 7
Ten Self-Defense Moves You Should Know

Obviously, you cannot become a skilled self-defense practitioner from a book, but any book on "total survival" would be incomplete without providing some basic physical self-defense information. In preparing this chapter, I sought the advice and help of some experienced martial arts practitioners. I wanted to show only those techniques that could easily be executed by a person of average age, build, and physical condition. It is certainly desirable for you to attend self-defense courses and even take up practical martial arts instruction. Such training requires constant maintenance and refresher courses to be effective. Most citizens face an assault situation with little or no training. Fortunately, most criminals are not trained martial arts experts. They are usually thugs who are looking for an easy target to harm or intimidate through brutal assault or restraint. They have the advantages of being accustomed to violence and having no misgivings about doing physical harm to another human being. They also have the advantage of choosing the place, direction, and method of the assault. Their first *action* will always be a bit faster than your *reaction*.

The one thing that the assailant is not expecting is instant and effective counteraction, followed by immediate disabling blows and kicks. If you are mentally prepared and have some basic moves programmed in your mind, you will go from denial to action fast enough to surprise the assailant and seize the initiative. In doing so, you have reversed the situation, but you cannot be content with just freeing yourself and waiting to see what he does next. You must disable the assailant while you still have a momentary advantage. If you hesitate, the situation is probably not going to end well for you. Put him down fast before he can recover.

The average citizen is usually repulsed by the idea of violence and doing harm to others. This gives the assailant the advantage of surprise and shock. The natural reaction to being grabbed is to pull away. The natural reaction to a knife or club assault is to turn and run, back away, or throw up your hands. The natural reaction to being choked is to try to pry the hands or arms away. The natural reaction to assault is to flail away with closed fists. None of these reactions will be effective in most cases.

The photographs that follow illustrate a few basic self-defense techniques that virtually anyone can implement. Looking at photos will not be enough to teach you these actions. Practicing with a partner until they become your new *natural* reactions and techniques is essential to true preparedness for this kind of situation. Of course, you must practice slowly step-by-step with care to avoid actual injury.

The Ten Principles Applied to Combat

In no situation are my ten principles of survival more applicable than before and during a physical combat situation. They are reviewed here as applied to these situations:

1. **Anticipate** a combat situation before it occurs when possible. Body language or demeanor indicating that someone may become combative or an environment where an assault is possible should have you in a state of readiness.
2. **Be aware** of your surroundings and those within striking distance. Have a mental plan for action related to the potential assault.
3. **Be there now** by focusing on your counterattack actions rather than letting any pain, injuries, or concerns about doing harm to another person slow you down.
4. **Staying calm** is always hard to do. The adrenaline rush usually works in your favor in combat, but it can give you tunnel vision where you miss other threats or run when you need to fight.
5. **Evaluate** your situation as you go and make decisions. Is there more than one assailant here? Is help coming? Is the assailant disabled enough that you can run away without being caught or do you need to use more strikes and kicks to end the threat?
6. **Doing the next right thing** in combat means following through on the first action with a series of strikes, kicks, and stomps with all your energy to end this situation.
7. **Taking control** is the first thing you must do immediately. Once you start applying basic self-defense techniques, the assailant is in a reactive mode, and you have started to take control. In your mind you must already be thinking that you are going to turn the tables and hurt this person.
8. **Have what you need** in terms of self-confidence, knowledge of basic techniques, and, if possible, self-defense equipment, such as a knife, collapsible baton, or other weapon.
9. **Using what you have** is a very good rule in combat. Employing keys, pens, or handy objects to strike, stab, or cut is important. You can also push the assailant over objects or bash his head against a solid object or a wall.
10. **Doing what is necessary** applies even more so in violent combat situations. You must overcome all reservations about kicking genitals, gouging eyes, stabbing with a pen, smashing teeth, and other nasty actions. You are a good person, and you deserve to survive. The assailant is unworthy of any consideration or mercy. Apply every technique with your full energy and speed.

Of course, the eleventh principle is "never give up," which is the most important of all the survival rules. In a combat situation, giving up means death or serious bodily injury. The techniques you try may not always work, or there may be multiple assailants. Lots of things can and probably will go wrong, but you keep moving and fighting. Giving up is not an option. Remember that combat situations seldom happen in nice, neat, open spaces. Walls, ledges, furniture, and other objects complicate the application of some techniques, but they can be used to your advantage if you keep your head and apply the ten principles.

1. PUSHING COUNTER

An assault can start when the aggressor attempts to push the victim, usually into an object or into a location advantageous to him. You could be pushed over a ledge, into a room, or against a wall as the first phase of an attack. Letting yourself be pushed is never advisable. If you are standing with both feet side by side facing the opponent, you will get pushed over. You must brace yourself with one foot back and at a forty-five-degree angle to the front foot. You can now pin the assailant's hand against your chest with one hand while leaning forward and bringing your arm down on his arm and twisting to push his trapped arm out and down. This will take him down while making it difficult for him to use his free arm against you. At this point, you are in a position to deliver a knee to the groin, an elbow to the face, a forearm to the face or neck, or to break the elbow by forcefully striking it from the rear while still holding the arm (see below).

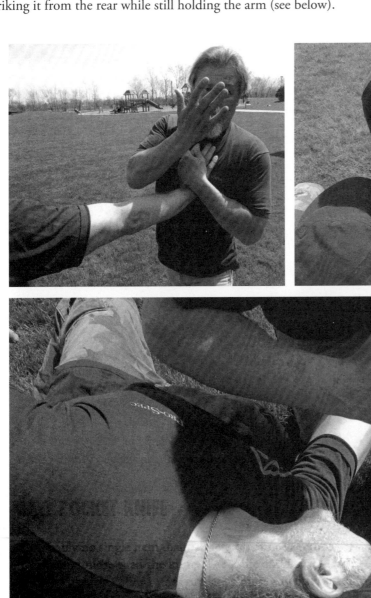

2. REAR-CHOKE COUNTER

A rear chokehold is a common method of assault. While there are many fancy and complex counters for this hold, most require that the defender be in good physical condition and at least moderately trained. The method shown here can be used by virtually anyone and is effective if delivered quickly and forcefully. You must stomp down as hard as possible on the top bridge of the assailant's foot, and repeat until you are released. If you can get your foot higher, kick at the shins and then scrape down and stomp the foot. Best of all, if you can deliver a forceful kick to the assailant's ankle, you can put him out of action. As soon as you are released, immediately kick at his knee or groin, and swing your elbow into his face. You can also forcefully bend back his finger or poke his eyes. These techniques are illustrated below.

3. FRONT-CHOKE COUNTER

Of course, it is best to avoid letting someone you don't know get this close to you, but if you are getting choked, you must act immediately before you start to lose consciousness. The assailant clearly intends to kill you, and you cannot hesitate to implement brutal countermeasures. Moving in and bringing the arms up relieves the pressure on the throat while putting you in range to gouge the eyes with the thumbs. Gripping the side of the face with the fingers, dig your thumbs into his eyes, trying to pop them out of the sockets. The assailant will quickly lose interest in choking you. Now is the time for a groin kick or fist to the side of his head or neck. Put him down!

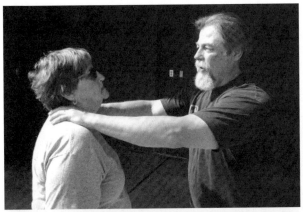

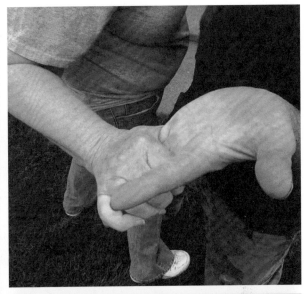

A good alternative to the eye gouge is to deliver a strong open-hand strike to the ear. This will rupture the eardrum and put the assailant out of the fight.

4. WRIST-HOLD COUNTER

An assault often starts with the assailant grabbing the victim's wrist. The expected reaction is for you to pull away. Rotating the arm out and down as shown below will break the assailant's grip. You have opened him up for forearm and elbow strikes, as well as groin and knee joint kicks.

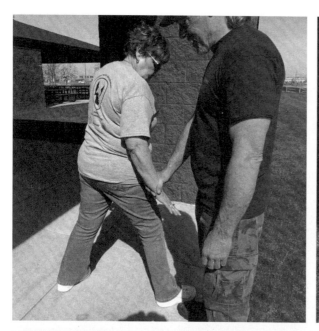
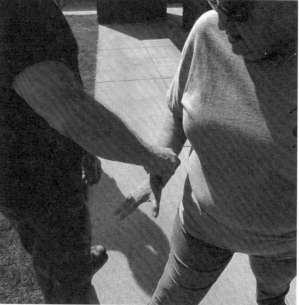
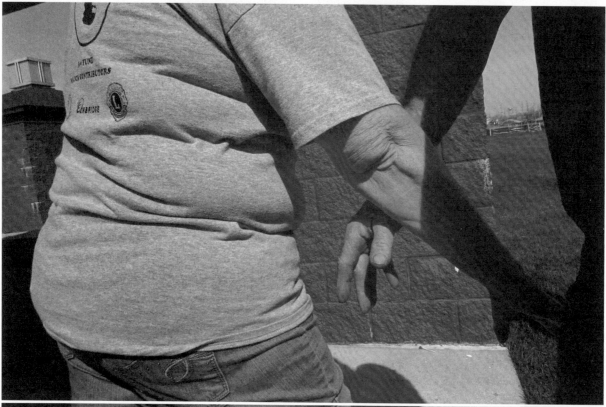

5. BODY-PINNED COUNTER

Having your body pinned down completely is probably the worst-case scenario in combat. You are on your back while the assailant has your arms pinned down with his legs, rendering you helpless to resist his blows and chokehold. As always, you need to act fast before you are beaten or choked to unconsciousness. Swing one leg over one of his legs as shown. Now rock and twist with all your strength in that direction, tipping the assailant over and reversing the situation. If done correctly and with force, you may break his ankle in the process. Quickly use a knee strike to the groin or kidneys while he is still surprised. The four images below illustrate these steps.

6. CLUB-ASSAULT COUNTER

Assailants often use blunt objects—such as pipes, bats, or sticks—as weapons. The natural reaction to such an assault is to move back or to try to use the arm as a defense. Since the club has more force at the far end as it is swung, the best defense is to close the distance to the assailant and initiate your own attacks, as shown below. A forearm to the throat while stepping in to push the assailant over makes his club ineffective. As always, additional blows to the face and neck together with groin kicks can finish the job. The follow-up moves to this action are the same as for a knife defense. The four images below illustrate these actions.

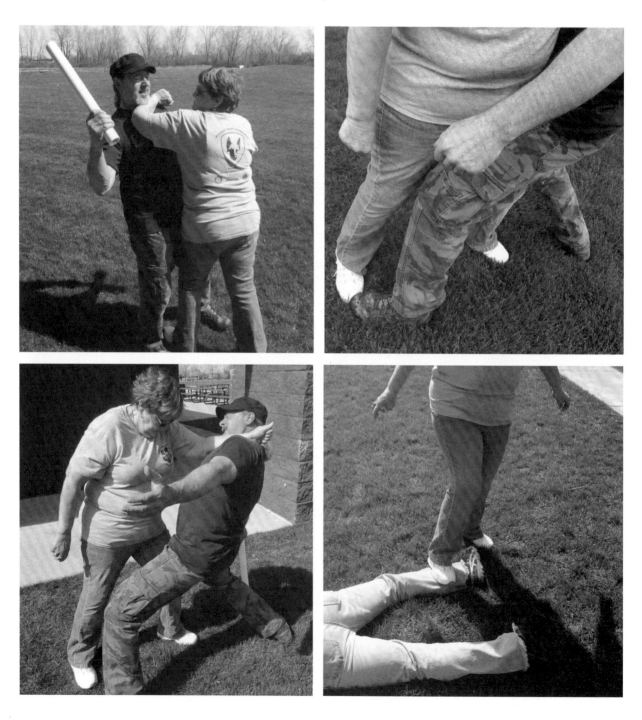

7. KNIFE-ATTACK DEFENSES

Being attacked by someone wielding a knife is frightening. Obviously, if you have any kind of weapon of your own, you are fully justified in using it. A chair can be used as a shield. Throwing rocks or using a pipe or stick as a club can be effective. But if you are caught unarmed facing an attacker with a knife, even the best defense will probably result in your being cut. If you are then distracted by the blood and pain, you will receive more cuts or be stabbed to death. While trained combat and martial arts practitioners have multiple counters for knife attacks, the average person's best chance (short of escape) is to step in close and fast, blocking the knife arm, and delivering disabling blows to the face and neck, and employing groin kicks.

Most knife assaults are from the underhand position, where the assailant holds the knife low, intending to make upward stabs to your abdomen. If you are pressed against the attacker, your vital organs are shielded by his body while you step inside to strike. Use your body to push him off balance while you deliver kicks and blows. Don't let him up. Put him on the ground, stomp on a knee or wrist, and kick his head or face.

The same principles apply to overhead knife assaults, as shown below. In all cases, the striking arm must be on the same side as the assailant's weapon (club or knife) to block it from effective use.

8. HANDGUN DEFENSES

Having a handgun pointed at you is probably the most serious situation you can be in. Before initiating any aggressive disarming procedures, you need to assess your chances of being shot. In the case of robbery, carjacking, and attempted abduction, running away may be the best option. FBI statistics show that only 2 percent of victims are actually shot at if they run and only 5 percent of those are actually hit. Even if you are shot while running, you still have a fair chance of survival. If the assailant clearly intends to shoot you, then the risk of attempting to disarm him may be justified. There is always a considerable risk in initiating a gun-disarming technique, and it is to be considered a last resort if no other hope of surviving is available. In each case you want to push the gun into a position where it can't be aimed at you and disable the attacker so that he either drops the gun or is effectively disabled.

Usually the assailant is behind you. In most cases he will be holding the weapon in his right hand, but you will be turning and stepping in and out of the line of fire regardless of what hand it's in. Turning your body quickly to the outside has the gun pointing past you before the assailant can pull the trigger. If the gun is fired, you cannot let the sound disrupt your actions. You continue to rotate behind the assailant, using the inside foot to trip him as you force him off balance and down. Stomping on an ankle, kidney, and wrist, hold the gun before he can roll over. The following eight images demonstrate these steps.

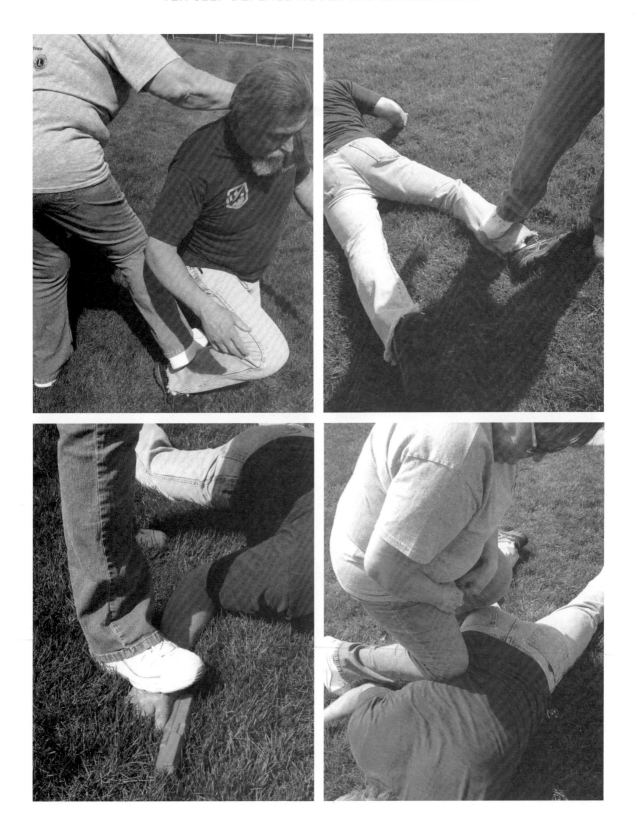

A gun to your head provides an opportunity to counter because you know where the gun and the assailant are at the start. Again, rotating and moving inward puts the gun over your shoulder before the opponent can pull the trigger. Keep in mind that the gun may go off next to your ear. Next you can gouge his eyes or kick his groin hard.

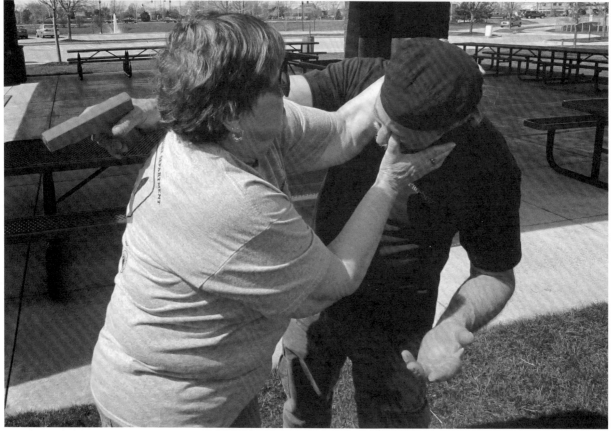

Alternatively or as follow-up, you can step in and twist the assailant's arm and fingers back and around to take him to the ground. Follow up immediately with disabling kicks.

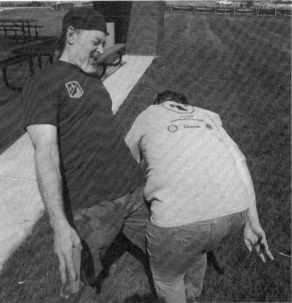

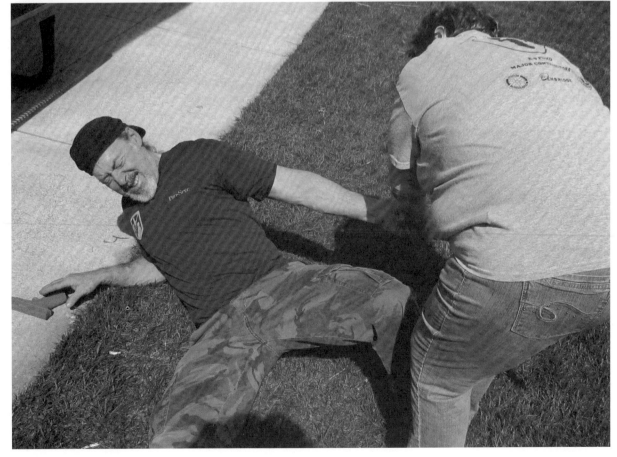

9. DISABLING STRIKES AND BLOWS

The fist is generally a poor striking object. The hand has many fragile bones, and the fist spreads the force over six square inches. A fist strike may hurt someone, but it seldom puts him down in one blow. The elbow and forearm are far better weapons. The elbow is sharp and can be used inside, where fist blows are ineffective. An elbow to the face, neck, groin, or kidney will quickly end the fight. An elbow to the sternum can also disable. Such blows must be delivered with a hard, twisting motion to maximize effect. The outside surface of the forearm provides a hard and focused striking surface. As shown in the photos below, such a strike can be effective against the face, throat, and back of the neck. Open-hand slaps can be used for the neck and groin, as well. You must step through the triangle between the opponent's legs as you deliver a strike to maximize the force.

Forearm blow to the side of neck

Forearm blow to the throat.

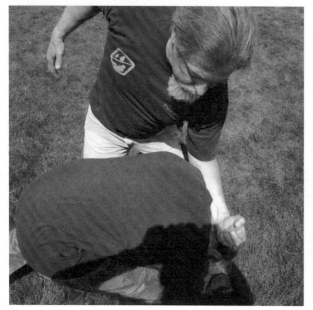

Elbow to sternum.

Open-hand strike to the throat.

Hit to the groin.

10. DISABLING KICKS AND STOMPS

The legs are far stronger than the arms and can deliver much greater force. When delivering a kick, use the movement and weight of the entire body in the direction of the kick. Don't kick *at* the target; kick through him. When using the knee to kick into the groin, kidney, or other point, use the body's full weight behind the strike. When kicking the groin, attempt to lift the opponent.

Kick to the groin.

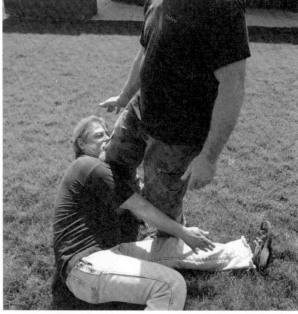

Knee to the face.

Stomp to the back.

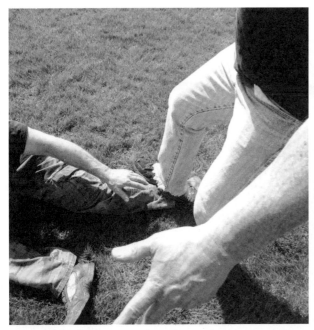

Stomp to the ankle.

Stomp to the knee.

Knee to the back.

CHAPTER 8
Ten Medical Skills You Should Know

The following skills are distilled from my twenty years as an emergency medical technician and as a developer and instructor for survival-medicine course materials. Here we will focus only on the basic skills and priorities for the recognition and immediate care of conditions that will either kill or permanently disable the patient and where lifesaving action does not require advanced skills or medical equipment. The first eight are critical lifesaving skills that cannot be delayed; effective bandaging and splinting relieve pain and prevent further complications and disabilities. These situations are easy to recognize, and the immediate steps needed to prevent death or disability are fairly easy for anyone to do.

1. OBSTRUCTED AIRWAY

Urgency: The first act in determining priorities in mass casualty situations is opening the airway to see whether the victim is breathing. The longer that the patient has not been breathing, the less likely he is to recover. Within five minutes of respiratory arrest, the heart will stop circulating blood and the brain will begin to suffer irreversible damages.

Recognition: In most cases respiratory arrest is the result of an airway obstruction that can be corrected by using the Heimlich maneuver or simply repositioning the head. The tongue may also create an obstruction in a prone patient.

Conscious with airway obstruction: The person will be unable to speak or cough forcefully and may give the universal sign of choking by placing a hand at the throat. There is no excuse for a person dying from this!

Unconscious or semiconscious: Person will be pale or blue, and unresponsive or gasping and wheezing.

Action: If you observe the patient choking before loss of consciousness, initiate the airway-clearing maneuver. If you find an apparently unconscious patient, shake the shoulders and shout, "Are you okay?" to awaken him. An unresponsive patient is a medical emergency. Call 911 or send someone to do so immediately before initiating further action. Tilt the head and lift the jaw to open the airway. Look at the chest, listen for sounds of breathing, and see if you can feel air on your cheek to determine if the person is breathing. Modern protocols eliminate the steps of abdominal thrusts for airway clearing, pulse checks, and rescue breathing. If the patient is not breathing with the head tilted as shown on the following page, initiate CPR immediately.

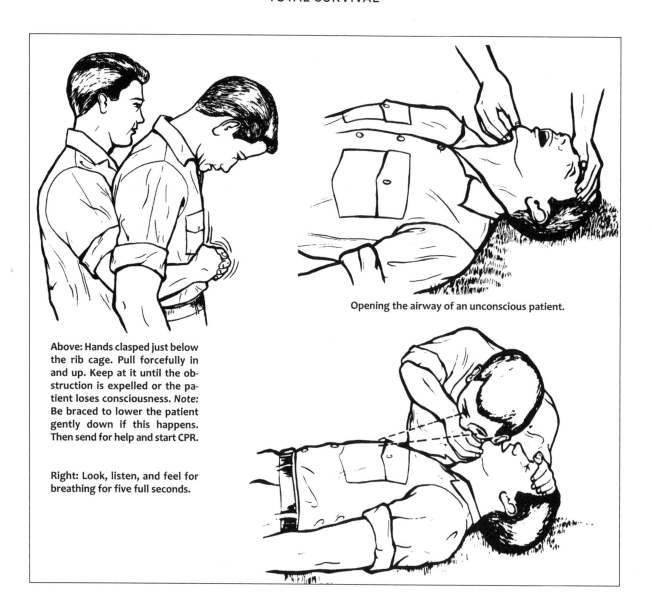

Opening the airway of an unconscious patient.

Above: Hands clasped just below the rib cage. Pull forcefully in and up. Keep at it until the obstruction is expelled or the patient loses consciousness. *Note:* Be braced to lower the patient gently down if this happens. Then send for help and start CPR.

Right: Look, listen, and feel for breathing for five full seconds.

2. CARDIAC ARREST (MYOCARDIAL INFARCTION)

Urgency: Better known as a "heart attack," myocardial infarctions (MI) result from obstruction of blood flow to heart tissue. This results in the death of tissue and a cessation of normal heart function. The heart goes into atrial fibrillation, which is a disorganized vibrating instead of beating. No blood is pumped and the body organs and brain begin to shut down. If the flow of oxygenated blood is not restored quickly, death is certain. Effective CPR can sustain life for a while but seldom results in restoring a normal cardiac rhythm and patient recovery. CPR provides a small chance at recovery and provides a savable patient for the EMS personnel or anyone who uses an Automatic External Defibrillator, AED. The sooner an AED is used, the better the chances of restoring the patient's heart rhythm.

Recognition: "Crushing" chest pains radiating to the back or left arm are classic signs of an MI. The patient may also be sweating, weak, dizzy, or even faint. The afflicted person may verbalize that they think they are going to die. If it might be a heart attack, act like it is a heart attack!

Action: Your first priority is to call 911 or send someone to do so. If the person is conscious, ask if they have prescription heart medication to take. Aspirin is a blood thinner and can reduce the severity of a heart attack. If the patient is not allergic to aspirin, taking two pills may be helpful.

CPR: The first course I took in CPR took eight hours. The current courses take about four hours. It should take about five minutes! No one has ever been saved by a certificate. If you can do what is described below, you can do CPR.

Instructions

1. Check for responsiveness.
2. Send for help.
3. Open airway, head tilt/chin lift or jaw thrust (no pulse check).
4. Initiate CPR.
5. Thirty hard compressions and two full breaths at a rate of 100 compressions per minute at the nipple line (a bit lower for children)
   - Compress chest 1.5 to 2 inches for adults (.5- to .75-inch for children). Use only one hand for children and just two to three fingers for an infant.
   - Hands interlocked, fingers up
   - Elbows locked
   - Weight directly over sternum
   - No bouncing or rocking
   - Thirty hard and fast compressions straight down (100 per minute)
   - Two full breaths (tilt the head, pinch the nose)
   - Continue until you are exhausted, the victim revives, or automated external defibrillator (AED) is started.

For two-person CPR: Use same count (thirty and two) and alternate between compressions and breathing, or take turns doing both.

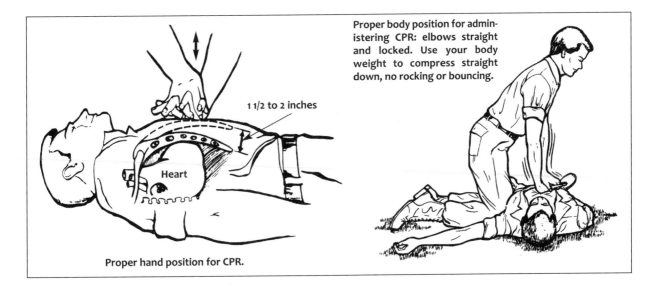

1 1/2 to 2 inches

Heart

Proper hand position for CPR.

Proper body position for administering CPR: elbows straight and locked. Use your body weight to compress straight down, no rocking or bouncing.

You Are Now Qualified to Do CPR

AED: I cannot say this more emphatically—anyone can and should use an AED immediately without hesitation on a patient whose heart has stopped. While AED training is desirable, it is not necessary. If you can use a cell phone, you are way overqualified to use an AED. If one is within reach, just open it up, push the button, and do what it tells you to do.

3. ARTERIAL BLEEDING (HYPOVOLEMIA)

Urgency: The normal blood volume for an adult (depending on size) is about six liters. The rapid loss of more than 10 percent of this volume will result in shock and then death within minutes. The blood delivers the oxygen and nutrients to the brain and body organs. Once blood volume and pressure drop, the brain, heart, and other organs cease to function, and death is immediate. Once the blood is lost, it cannot be replaced fast enough to recover the damage without intravenous fluids (IV) and transfusions.

Recognition: Arterial bleeding is marked by pressurized spraying of bright red blood that squirts with each heartbeat. It does not take long for the heart to pump out enough blood to result in death.

Action: You only have seconds! Apply direct pressure with your bare hand on top of the injury. Elevate the bleeding limb. If a cloth dressing (T-shirts, anything) is available, apply it with pressure. If blood soaks through, add more dressings on top, but do not remove the original dressing. If direct pressure fails to stop the bleeding or the patient must be moved or moves on his own, apply a tourniquet, as shown below. A tourniquet is seldom needed below the elbow or knee. Be sure it is visible and mark "TK" and the time applied on the victim's forehead.

The tourniquet should be applied at least one to two inches wide to prevent cutting into the skin and should be applied about two inches above the wound. After bleeding is controlled, the injured extremity should be splinted to prevent further bleeding, even if no fracture is present.

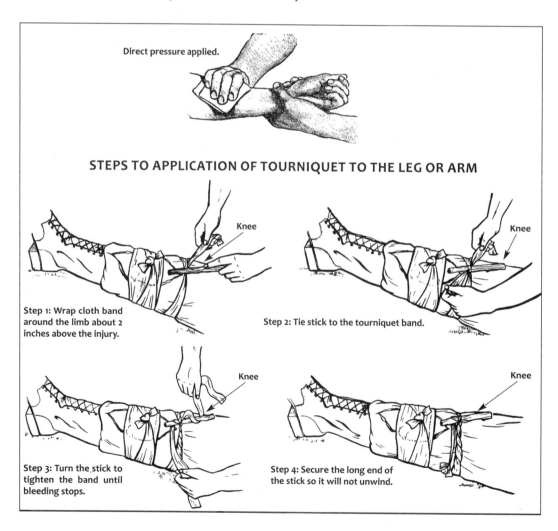

Direct pressure applied.

STEPS TO APPLICATION OF TOURNIQUET TO THE LEG OR ARM

Step 1: Wrap cloth band around the limb about 2 inches above the injury.

Step 2: Tie stick to the tourniquet band.

Step 3: Turn the stick to tighten the band until bleeding stops.

Step 4: Secure the long end of the stick so it will not unwind.

Knee

4. HEAT STROKE (HYPERTHERMIA)

Urgency: Heat stroke is an immediate, life-threatening condition. The victim has probably gone through heat exhaustion (e.g., profuse sweating, weakness, dizziness), which is a mild form of hypovolemic shock and has now progressed to full hypovolemia. If the patient is not cooled and rehydrated immediately, the condition may be irreversible.

Recognition: The patient who has been working/exercising under hot conditions for an extended period is at risk for heat stroke. Adequate hydration and frequent rest breaks are effective ways to prevent this life-threatening condition. Heat stroke exhibits when the patient no longer sweats and the skin becomes red and dry. Weakness, thirst, nausea, dizziness, slurred speech, and even diminished levels of awareness may be present.

Action: Immediate cooling is the only chance to save this patient. Apply cold packs or cold wet towels to the neck, armpits, and groin areas. If possible, immerse forearms or the whole body in cold water. If patient is conscious, provide something cold to drink. If available, provide a sports drink to supply needed electrolytes. *Cool the patient now!* Of course, once he starts to recover, cease aggressive cooling efforts to prevent hypothermia.

5. EXPOSURE (HYPOTHERMIA)

Urgency: Uncontrollable shivering is the final effort of the body to maintain temperature. Prolonged exposure to cold and wet conditions, such as exercising in cold weather, can use up the body's reserves of energy and lead to the fast onset of hypothermia once the activity is stopped. If hypothermia has progressed too far, the body's ability to reheat shuts down. The temperature of a hypothermic patient brought into a warm (75-degree) room will continue to drop and could lead to death unless internal and external heat sources are applied. Prevention and early recognition and treatment are essential here.

Recognition: After prolonged exposure to cold or cool, wet conditions, the patient ceases to shiver and becomes less responsive, and coordinated hypothermia is evident. Slurred speech, staggering gait, and diminished levels of alertness and awareness are sure signs of advancing hypothermia, which will lead to unconsciousness and then death.

Action: First, remove the patient from the cold environment and remove all cold, wet clothing. Warming a patient with advanced hypothermia too fast can force the cold blood from the extremities to circulate to the heart, causing fibrillation and death. A combination of slow external and internal warming is recommended. If the patient is conscious, providing warm, sweet drinks that warm from the inside is the best treatment, combined with warm packs around the neck and blankets in a warm environment. Yes, putting the patient into a sleeping bag with another person is effective if no warm cabin or vehicle is available.

6. SUCKING CHEST WOUND (PNEUMOTHORAX)

Urgency: When the chest wall is punctured, air begins to enter the pleural space between the inner chest wall and the lungs. With each breath, the space fills with more air and compresses the lungs further. The lungs are pushed and squeezed smaller and smaller. In addition, the heart may be compressed, and blood (hemothorax) may also fill the pleural spaces. Eventually the patient is unable to breathe at all and will suffocate. Fast action can markedly improve the patient's chances for survival.

Recognition: Look for a hole in the chest wall that is emitting air and usually some foamy blood. Locate the cause, and remember that there may be a hole in the back as well. If so, both holes will need to be closed, as shown below. The patient will experience growing difficulty in breathing. The trachea in the neck may shift away from the injured side as the lungs are forced away, and the skin will be pale or bluish in color.

Action: Use anything that is airtight—such as cellophane, plastic wrap, or foil—to cover the hole. Be sure the covering is large enough not to be sucked into the hole. Tape over the wound on all four sides. Secure the cover in place and roll the patient onto his injured side. Note: If the patient's breathing difficulties get worse, you must remove the seal.

This is the simple and fastest procedure. Some medical protocols call for leaving a corner of the cover/seal open to act as a one-way valve flap.

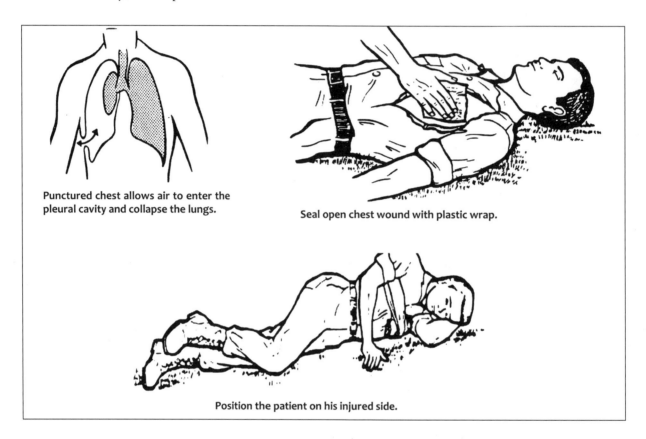

Punctured chest allows air to enter the pleural cavity and collapse the lungs.

Seal open chest wound with plastic wrap.

Position the patient on his injured side.

7. SHOCK

In most of the above cases, death ultimately results from hypovolemic shock. Shock can result from any of the conditions above. Shock is caused by an inadequate cellular profusion of oxygen, which is a result of:

- Not enough oxygen in the blood because of respiratory arrest or collapsed lungs
- Not enough blood pressure to force oxygen into the cells caused by cardiac arrest, blood loss, or dehydration from burns, heat exposure, or prolonged illness

Urgency: In the early stages of shock, the body will attempt to compensate (compensated shock) by vascular contraction and increased heart rate and respirations. The patient's level of consciousness may appear normal until the compensation fails and the patient "crashes" into uncompensated shock and death. In the absence of IV fluids and oxygen, it is nearly impossible to reverse uncompensated shock. The patient's survival can only be supported by immediately treating the cause (e.g., bleeding, dehydration) and initiating treatment procedures to reduce the effects.

Recognition: Expect shock anytime severe bleeding or dehydration is evident. The first signs of shock are restlessness and anxiety, followed by a weakening and rapid pulse, cold moist skin, sweating, pale or bluish skin, thirst, lusterless eyes, nausea, vomiting, and declining level of consciousness.

Action: You must stop any severe bleeding, heat exposure, and respiratory or cardiac issues immediately. Get the patient into a prone position with the feet elevated about twelve inches to facilitate blood flow to the vital organs. Keep the patient warm but not hot. In general, it is not advisable to provide fluids if professional medical care (IV fluids) will be available. Moistening the lips is permissible. However, if no further help is available and the patient is conscious and will tolerate oral fluids, consider initiating the dehydration treatment below.

8. SEVERE DEHYDRATION

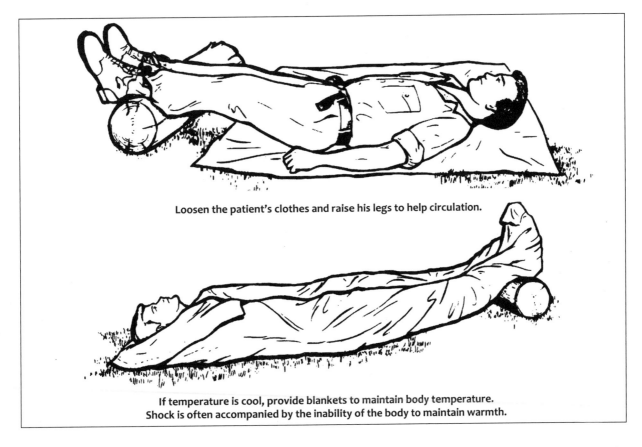

Loosen the patient's clothes and raise his legs to help circulation.

If temperature is cool, provide blankets to maintain body temperature.
Shock is often accompanied by the inability of the body to maintain warmth.

Urgency: Dehydration is one of the primary causes of death secondary to shock, heat stroke, radiation sickness, severe bleeding, burns, prolonged illness, chemical agent exposure, and anything else that causes more fluid loss than can be replaced. While dehydration does not happen immediately, it is often the cause of death from other conditions. In the absence of IV fluid administration, dehydration is difficult to reverse once the patient's level of consciousness or ability to swallow is compromised. Prompt recognition of the danger and constant hydration maintenance can significantly improve the patient's ability to survive and recover from a serious injury or illness.

Recognition: Pinch the skin on the back of the patient's hand. If it does not immediately recover, there is evidence of dehydration. Pale skin, weakness, sunken eyes, thirst, nausea, and headache are all signs of dehydration. Anyone who has been exposed to high temperatures, has been vomiting, or has had diarrhea and profuse sweating will probably be dehydrated if not frequently rehydrated. Dark yellow urine or low urine output (below 90 ccs in two hours) is a sign of dehydration.

Action: The potential for shock can be reduced by attention to hydration. A well-hydrated body will tolerate blood loss and fluid loss better to begin with. In the absence of IV fluids, rehydration is difficult. If ambulance and ER treatment are not immediately available and the patient is fully conscious, oral hydration can be sustained using the following solution.

Rehydration Solution

- Six teaspoons of sugar
- One teaspoon of salt to one liter of water
- Provide a four-ounce drink every hour

Caution: Giving water or other liquids to an unconscious, semiconscious, or seriously injured patient may cause him to vomit and aspirate, resulting in pneumonia. Generally these patients can be rehydrated by intravenous methods at the ER only.

9. BASIC BANDAGING

Lacerations, abrasions, and burns are common injuries, and they are almost guaranteed to happen during a survival situation. These "soft tissue" injuries must be cleaned and bandaged effectively to relieve pain, prevent infection, and allow the injured person to continue functioning. In a survival setting, only the walking, working wounded will be able to survive. You may not have all the prepackaged, self-adhesive bandaging products that we all now take for granted. You may need to use triangles and strips of clean or preferably sterile cloths for bandaging. Dressings may be secured with medical tape, Saran Wrap, duct tape, or electrical tape. Here are the basic procedures for bandaging and a few illustrated examples:

- If the wound is bleeding heavily, your only priority is to stop the bleeding.
- Freely bleeding wounds should be covered with a sterile dressing bandaged in place.
- Abrasions and shallow wounds should be cleaned with soap and water and covered with a sterile dressing.
- For skin flaps: flush with clean water and replace flap before applying dressing.
- For separated skin: apply dressing to wound and keep skin dry and cool for reattachment.
- A sterile dressing is preferred, but a clean dressing is better than no dressing.
- Washing with soap and water is adequate for cleaning wounds. Alcohol, iodine, and other agents are not recommended.
- Dirty wounds can be flushed with clean water or saline (salt) solution from a squirt bottle.
- Extensive cleaning and debridement (removal of debris from a wound) should be avoided unless medical care is unavailable.

10. BASIC SPLINTING

Splinting is not casting. It is intended to reduce the movement of bone ends or joints until the bones can be reset and a cast can be applied. Fractures that present with deformity of the limb or open wounds are particularly serious and require prompt and advanced medical attention. Nondisplaced fractures may be transported with less urgency. In general, splinting requires two people: one person holds the injured limb while the other carefully applies the splint.

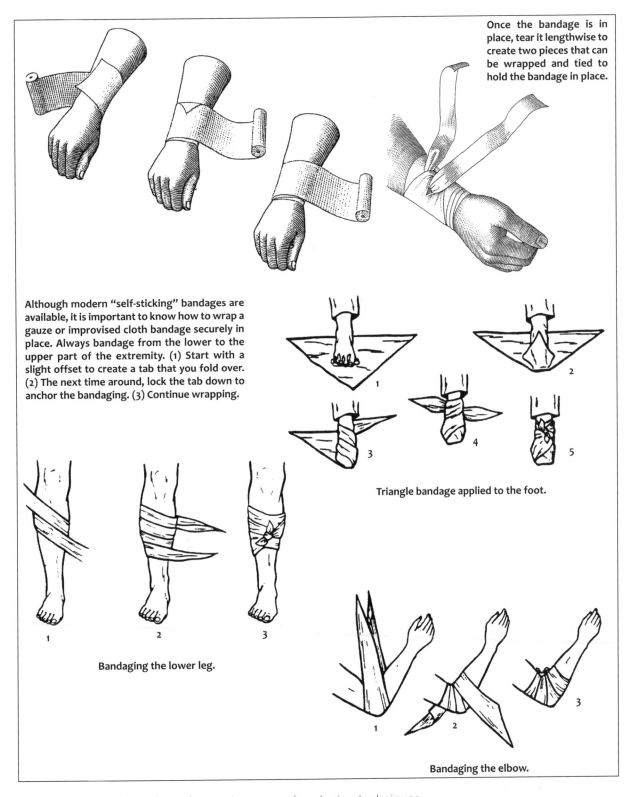

Once the bandage is in place, tear it lengthwise to create two pieces that can be wrapped and tied to hold the bandage in place.

Although modern "self-sticking" bandages are available, it is important to know how to wrap a gauze or improvised cloth bandage securely in place. Always bandage from the lower to the upper part of the extremity. (1) Start with a slight offset to create a tab that you fold over. (2) The next time around, lock the tab down to anchor the bandaging. (3) Continue wrapping.

Triangle bandage applied to the foot.

Bandaging the lower leg.

Bandaging the elbow.

The illustrations above show the most common bandaging techniques.

Recognition of Dislocations and Fractures

Fractures and dislocations are usually the result of trauma from a fall, collision, impact, or strenuous action. Indications of such injuries include pain at the site, discoloration, inability to move the limb, swelling, and deformity. If in doubt, compare the injured limb to the uninjured one. That should confirm these signs. A suspected strain or sprain should be splinted and treated as a fracture until proven otherwise. Always check for a pulse and sensation below the injury after splinting; if circulation has been compromised, remove the splint, reposition the limb, and reapply the splint.

SPLINTING PROCEDURES

- Check for pulse and feeling and movement below the fracture. If there is no pulse, the victim is in danger of losing the limb.
- If there is an open fracture where bone is exposed (visible or not), stop the bleeding and cover the wound before splinting.
- Splint the fracture or dislocation in the position you found it. Do not attempt to realign or reduce it, as moving bones or joints may damage nerves and cut blood vessels, resulting in further injury.
- Only in cases where there is no pulse below the fracture before or after splinting and no hope of prompt medical attention should you try realigning the bones enough to restore the pulse.
- Use anything that will keep the bone or joint from moving (e.g., newspapers, magazines, boards, blankets).
- If nothing else is available, splint the injured limb to the body or uninjured adjoining limb.
- For fractures, you must immobilize the joint on either side of the fractured bone.
- For dislocations, splint from the bone on one side to the bone on the other side of the joint.
- Always check the pulse below the fracture before and after splinting methods.

Conclusion

Applying bandages, splints, and other treatments for injuries is important, but the recognition and immediate treatment of the first eight above conditions are the most important life-saving actions that you can and must

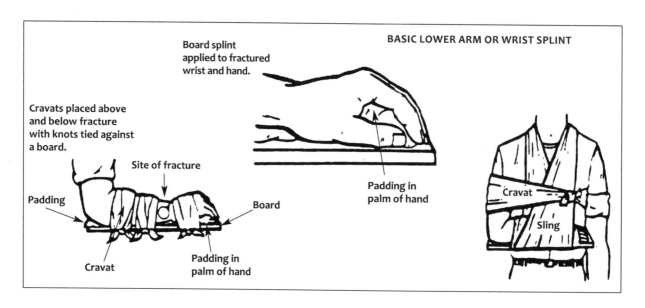

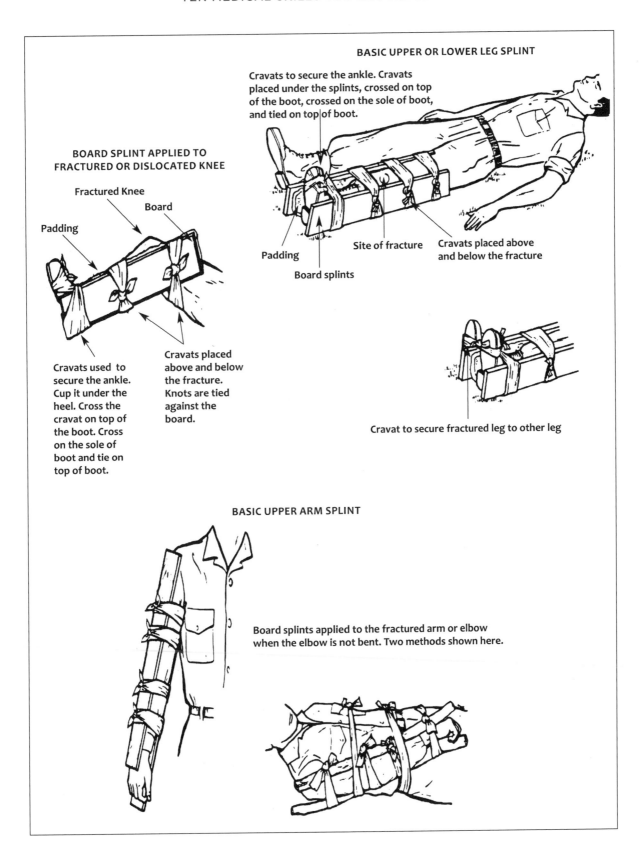

BASIC UPPER OR LOWER LEG SPLINT

Cravats to secure the ankle. Cravats placed under the splints, crossed on top of the boot, crossed on the sole of boot, and tied on top of boot.

BOARD SPLINT APPLIED TO FRACTURED OR DISLOCATED KNEE

Fractured Knee

Board

Padding

Cravats used to secure the ankle. Cup it under the heel. Cross the cravat on top of the boot. Cross on the sole of boot and tie on top of boot.

Cravats placed above and below the fracture. Knots are tied against the board.

Padding

Board splints

Site of fracture

Cravats placed above and below the fracture

Cravat to secure fractured leg to other leg

BASIC UPPER ARM SPLINT

Board splints applied to the fractured arm or elbow when the elbow is not bent. Two methods shown here.

apply. With these you can save most lives from immediate death and give the individual a chance for further treatment and recovery.

Failure to act in these cases is almost always disastrous. Having read this, you have no excuse for letting that happen on your watch.

Addendum: Improvised Medical Techniques and Formulas

Dakin's Solution

Dakin's solution can be used to soak dressings for shallow wounds and flush deep wounds while healing. It was used to reduce gangrene during World Wars I and II, before penicillin was available.

1. Boil four cups of clean water for fifteen minutes.
2. Add one-half teaspoon of baking soda and let cool.
3. Add three ounces of bleach.
4. Store in sealed container protected from light.

Saline (Salt) Solution

Saline solution can be used to flush wounds and maintain bandage moisture. Make a 100-percent saline solution by adding one teaspoon of salt slowly to two cups of warm water and mixing. When the salt starts to settle to the bottom instead of mixing, it is 100-percent saturated. Pour off the solution from the settled crystals. You can now mix this with sterile water to make 50, 20, or any other percentage of saline solution you need. "Normal" saline is 9 percent.

Water Purification

Eight to sixteen drops of bleach per gallon.

Decontamination (Spray-Wash) Solution

Ten-percent bleach-water solution.

Super Glue

Super Glue can be used to close shallow wounds but not deep wounds.

Saran Wrap

Plastic wrap can be used to bandage large wounds and hold dressings and splints in place.

CHAPTER 9
Ten Ways to Gather and Purify Water

Wars have been fought over access to water sources, and whole cultures have risen and fallen with the flow of rivers and springs. Water supplies are major targets for terrorists and are vulnerable to all manner of natural and man-made disaster. Not only will safe water be critical to your family's survival, it could be a more valuable trade commodity than food or medicine. The water pumps are the heart of urban/suburban civilization. During a white-out, they would die in a matter of days. Compared to water, oil is hardly significant. Truly, he who controls the water controls life, and he who has his own water is free.

Depending on age, health, level of activity, and environmental factors (e.g., temperature, humidity), the average person can only survive about three days without water. The average person under normal conditions requires at least one quart of drinking water per day. When reasonable sanitation and cooking needs are added, a minimum of one gallon per day is a more practical rule of thumb for emergency storage.

1. STORING WATER

Although, in theory, you can never store too much water, it is heavy and takes up a lot of room. If you anticipate that you will be staying at home and that your home will be safe from fire, floods, and other conditions, then you can store your water there. If, however, your home could be damaged or inaccessible, you should consider storing water in a safer but reachable location. Consider whether you may need to carry your water. A fifty-five-gallon drum of water in your basement would be of no use if you have to evacuate. Plastic containers that were designed to hold water, juice, or soft drinks are good for storing water. Milk containers can be used but are flimsy and hard to get clean. Never use containers that originally held soaps, solvents, or other chemicals. Containers should be rinsed thoroughly with clean water and then soaked in a mild (10-percent) bleach solution. As soon as you dump out the solution, fill the container with clean water and seal tightly. Most municipal water can be stored without additional treatment. If you are storing well water or other types of water you are unsure about, add 6 or 8 drops of household bleach to each gallon. Of course, you may simply want to buy bottled water at the store. Five gallons of stored water per person should be sufficient for most basic short-term emergencies. (See Chapter 3, "Ten Items for the Prepared Home.")

If you have an early warning that there may be a water shortage, you should collect as much water as possible while it is still flowing. Fill your bathtub, sinks, pans, and other containers. Also fill your washing machine but do not add soap, as well as any children's wading pools and tote bins that may be available.

2. SCAVENGING FOR WATER

If you have failed to store enough water or you find yourself in a location where no stored water is available, you may need to use water from other sources. Not all these sources are drinkable, but they may provide water for other needs. If you have your own well, you have the water problem solved if you have a backup power supply for the pump. If not, get one. The toilet flush tank (not the bowl) contains several gallons of clean, drinkable water. Do not flush the toilet with this clean water. Scoop it out and use it for drinking and cooking. You can flush the toilet with dirty brown water from washing or with water that is unsafe for drinking. Your water heater contains a lot of clean water. Turn off the main water and gas valves and drain the twenty to sixty gallons of good water from the tank. Water pipes in a building contain gallons of water after the supply has stopped. Turn off the main valve to prevent drain-back and contamination, and drain the system from the lowest faucet, usually the laundry room sink.

Swimming pools and garden ponds can hold hundreds of gallons of water. In fact, they may be considered as family emergency water reservoirs. Properly maintained swimming pool water may be used for drinking and cooking, but the chlorine content will affect the taste. Even a small pool will supply lots of water for cleaning and flushing. If left uncovered, they can be contaminated with airborne biological, chemical, and radioactive materials. Most biological contaminants can be killed by boiling (a rolling boil for three to four minutes). Nuclear fallout can be removed through filtration. Decorative garden ponds may contain debris, animal and bird feces, and other contaminants, so water from them would require filtration, bleach treatment, or boiling before use.

Many homes have a sump pit and a sump pump in the basement. These function to pump away ground water seepage before it can flood the basement. Ground water in populated areas is not like well water and is often contaminated. A prudent homeowner would have a battery-powered backup pump or a generator to ensure that this pump will run during a power outage. If your city water supply is gone, so is your electricity, so you will need to pump or bail this water out regularly. This can be a supply of water for flushing, cleaning, or watering plants. As a last resort, you could filter, bleach, or boil this water for drinking.

You can assume that water taken directly from rivers, lakes, and marshes is polluted and must be decontaminated. Water from lakes that is taken well away from shore and away from discharge points may be safe. Ground water taken near the surface of a flood plain and away from inhabited areas is probably safe, as is water from most springs. Water from desert waterholes and just beneath the surface of vegetation patches in the desert is usually pure. Snow and rain are pure if gathered before contact with ground or contaminated services. There are exceptions to all of these, so filter and purify whenever possible.

Note: If there is dead vegetation or animals near a desert waterhole, it may contain poisonous chemicals. Do not drink!

3. COLLECTING WATER

In the old days people directed water from gutters into rain barrels to gather water for home use. Large plantations had cisterns to collect rainwater in the wet months for use in the dry times. Rain on a house roof during one storm can provide enough water for weeks. Even dew and frost melting into the gutters can produce several quarts of water each morning. Consider retrofitting gutter piping to divert water into containers. The water will be contaminated, but it can be filtered, bleached, or boiled for use.

Rivers and streams today are almost always contaminated. Even in wilderness areas, animal feces and carcasses upstream may pollute the seemingly clean water. Consider open stream and drainage ditches as a last resort. As is, it can be used for watering plants and fire protection. If you have no other alternative, you can filter, beach, or boil it for washing and drinking. Beware of water sources that have no plants growing near them, have odd smells or colorations, or are near dead animals. These sources may contain man-made or natural (e.g., arsenic) contamination that cannot be easily removed.

The so-called "desert still" was designed to distill small amounts of water from seemingly dry desert soil and cactus pieces in an emergency. This same system can be used to distill much more water from moist soil and foliage. A similar still can be constructed to render drinkable water from saltwater, as illustrated below.

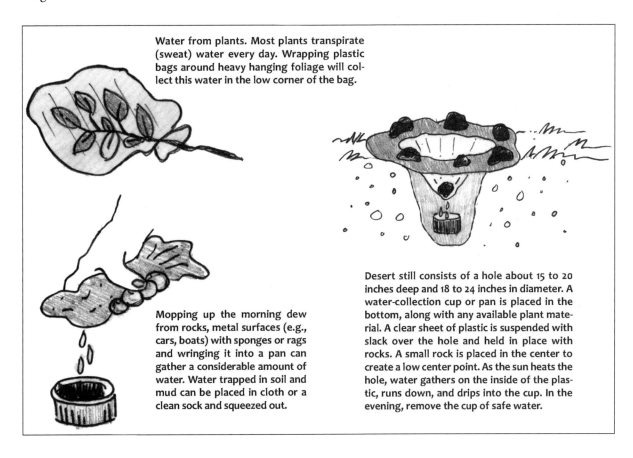

Water from plants. Most plants transpire (sweat) water every day. Wrapping plastic bags around heavy hanging foliage will collect this water in the low corner of the bag.

Mopping up the morning dew from rocks, metal surfaces (e.g., cars, boats) with sponges or rags and wringing it into a pan can gather a considerable amount of water. Water trapped in soil and mud can be placed in cloth or a clean sock and squeezed out.

Desert still consists of a hole about 15 to 20 inches deep and 18 to 24 inches in diameter. A water-collection cup or pan is placed in the bottom, along with any available plant material. A clear sheet of plastic is suspended with slack over the hole and held in place with rocks. A small rock is placed in the center to create a low center point. As the sun heats the hole, water gathers on the inside of the plastic, runs down, and drips into the cup. In the evening, remove the cup of safe water.

Amish home with gutters routed to basement cistern. A pump in the kitchen brings the water to the sink.

Typical rain barrel water-collection system.

4. FINDING WATER

Locating water in many areas is not difficult. Following the slope of the land downhill gets you closer to the water table and streams. Heavier foliage indicates surface or near-surface water. Even in the desert, outcroppings of vegetation may signal subsurface water, or the vegetation may be used in a water still. The barrel cactus will contain a spongy pulp containing water. The diagram below illustrates some typical water sources.

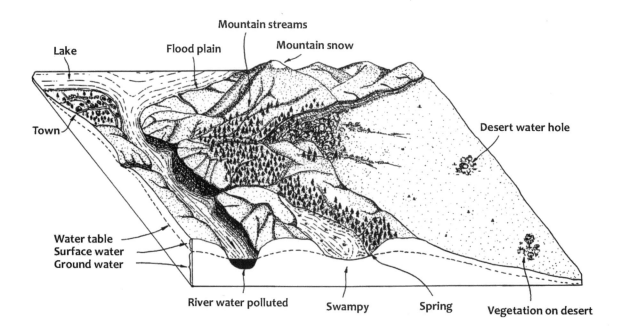

Certain species of barrel cactus may be a source of water in the desert. Photo credit: Wikipedia/Stan Shebs.

5. CHEMICAL PURIFICATION

The two most common methods of water purification are chlorine bleach and iodine. Household bleach contains about 8 percent chlorine so six to eight drops per gallon are recommended, but bleach loses strength over time so ten drops per gallon, especially if the water is cloudy, may be a safer choice. Tincture of iodine is another good method of purification and is particularly recommended for use in southern and tropical environments. Add five drops of 2-percent USP tincture of iodine to a quart of clear water or ten drops to cloudy water. Mix in the bleach or iodine and let it stand for an hour before drinking. Chlorine and iodine water-purification tablets are available from camping supply outlets for about five dollars for a fifty-tablet bottle. These small bottles can be carried in pockets and survival kits. These come with clear instructions for use

6. BOILING WATER TO PURIFY

Bringing water to a vigorous boil for at least three full minutes will kill biological contaminants and some chemical contaminants as well. You can add a pinch of salt or pour the water back and forth to aerate it to restore taste. This is the most effective and practical method of purification if fuel is not a problem.

7. DISTILLATION OF WATER

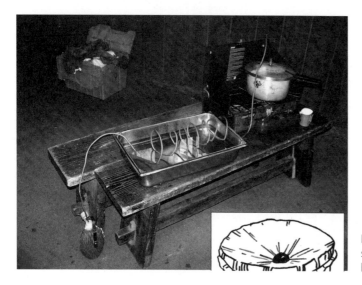

Left: Distillation can also be done using a solar still as shown. This process is slower, but it requires no fuel.

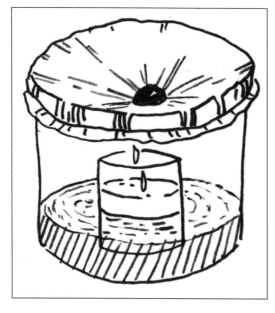

Left: A simple solar still made from a round pan or bucket and clear plastic. Place a cup (weighted, so it won't float) in the center and pour saltwater in the pan. The sun will distill the water (minus the salt) into the cup.

Boiling water into steam and then condensing it into clean water provides water free of biological and particulate contaminants. Even saltwater can be distilled into drinkable water. *Note:* Some volatile chemical contaminants may remain in the distilled water. Distilled water often tastes flat; shaking it to aerate will restore a normal water taste. If you suspect serious chemical contamination, don't try this method.

Stills can be improvised but having the components ready and tested is better yet. A still system consists of the following:

- Heat sources, such as a stove or fire.
- A closed tank or pot in which to boil the contaminated water.
- A long tube or coil to trap the steam and cool it.
- The tub can be cooled by air (coiling) or water. Wrap the coil in cloth kept wet.
- A container to catch the water.

8. WATER FILTRATION AND PURIFICATION SYSTEMS

Filtrating canteen with the filter built into the cap.

Commercially made water-filtration systems come in a variety of sizes and price ranges, and can filter thousands of gallons of water for home use.

Homemade filter using alternating layers of sand and activated charcoal separated by coffee filters. After filtration, use bleach for biological decontamination of rainwater from the roof.

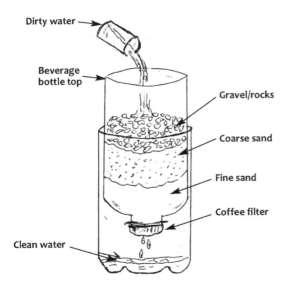

This filter uses a large plastic beverage bottle with the top cut off and inverted. The top layer is clean gravel, followed by coarse sand and then fine sand held in place by a coffee filter.

There are too many commercial water-purification systems to cover here. Pocket-sized LifeStraw systems capable of filtering several hundred gallons of water sell for about twenty dollars. There are also filtration bottles where you put unfiltered water in and squeeze filtered water out. Larger portable systems able to filter up to 4,000 to 5,000 gallons can be bought for less than a hundred dollars. Large units for the home that can remove 99.999 percent of bacteria and chemicals at a rate of ten gallons or more per day can be found for a few hundred dollars. One of the first steps to true preparedness is to get a larger filtration system for the home and a smaller one for your evacuation pack.

Water-filtering canteens and water bottles are available at sporting goods stores or survival stores for about thirty to forty dollars. Additional filters run from twenty to thirty dollars. Definitely must-haves, these are more practical for evacuation packs and short-term situations than long-term shelter-in-place use.

Note: The best source for clean gravel, clean sand, and activated charcoal is an aquarium supply store.

9. ULTRAVIOLET PURIFICATION

Ultraviolet (UV) light has been used for municipal water purification since the 1940s. UV light destroys microorganisms that cause diseases through the process of thymine dimerization. In recent years UV light water-purification systems have become available to the public for home use and the outdoors. UV devices use very little energy and do not involve adding chemicals to the water. UV light kills biological contamination but does not remove chemical and particulate contamination, so filtration is still necessary if these kinds of contaminants are present. Home systems can cost from a few hundred to a few thousand dollars. Portable, pocket-sized UV water purifiers cost from fifty dollars to a few hundred dollars and can be rechargeable.

Ultraviolet light from the sun can be used to purify water. You must know that the source water is not chemically contaminated, as UV will not remove chemicals. Natural sunlight will kill microorganisms just as the UV light devices do. You need to start out with a clean, clear (no color) plastic bottle (shown on previous page). Do not use glass, as it blocks the UV penetration. Fill the bottle with water and place it in direct sunlight. Place the bottle on its side with the long side facing the sun to maximize exposure. For improved results, place the bottle on a reflective surface, such as a white board or aluminum foil. Leave the bottle exposed for at least six hours on a mostly sunny day; if it is partly cloudy on that day, you may need to leave the water exposed for up to two days to ensure effective decontamination.

10. WATER CONSERVATION

Water that is unsafe to drink may be okay for washing clothes or watering plants. Water that has been used for washing or is from an unsafe source can still be used to flush the toilet. Try not to use drinking water for anything but drinking, food washing, hand washing, and medical care. Use recycled water for noncontact applications or decontaminate it through filtration and purification if possible. Once the emergency situation starts, you have to gather every drop you can and make every drop count. Stay hydrated, my friend.

CHAPTER 10
Ten Ways to Gather and Store Food

Next to air and water, food is the most important survival necessity. In theory, most healthy people can get by without much food for several weeks or longer, but serious physiological and psychological effects take place within a few days that can ultimately lead to other survival hazards. The lack of nutrition compromises the body's immune system, ability to heal, and capacity to stay warm. Being hungry is an unsafe mental state that leads the victim to make unsafe decisions. The mind fixated on food lacks awareness and alertness necessary to avoid other hazards. Lastly, individuals who are forced to take desperate measures to acquire food become a danger to themselves and all around them. For these reasons, you should have enough stored food for anticipated emergencies and the skills to safely find, create, and store more food if the situation is extended. Most households have a few weeks' worth of food around before they go into survival mode. The methods that follow include ways to expand food stockpiles and ways to acquire sustainable food supplies.

1. STOCKING UP AND STORING

The most common method of ensuring that you have food when you need it is stocking up and storing it. In the short term it is faster and cheaper, and takes less work than other methods. For home survival, where weight and space are not a big issue, the best method is to simply stock up on various canned goods and staples (e.g., sugar, honey, flour, rice, legumes) and rotate them into use. Most of these items last at least a few years, so you can have a year's supply of food without ever having any food in stock more than a year old. Several preparedness supply companies actually provide foods and storage racks for such systems. Where space is limited or weight is an issue, freeze-dried foods are more practical. These are more expensive but keep much longer, and you can carry a lot more food if you need to evacuate. You do need to have a lot of safe water and fuel for heating it to reconstitute these products.

The Food and Drug Administration (FDA) recommends 2,000 calories per day for anyone over four years old. This is for a *normal* person under *normal* conditions Stress, physical labor, and cold weather can dramatically increase nutritional needs. The FDA recommends fifty grams of protein and 300 grams of carbohydrates. There are also specific recommendations and limits for sugar, sodium, cholesterol, fiber, minerals, and vitamins. In fact, the percentage of recommended fat (<65 grams), saturated fat (<20 grams), cholesterol (<300 grams), sodium (<2,400 milligrams), potassium (3,500 milligrams), and total carbohydrates (300 grams) per 2,000-calorie-per-day diet is listed on every food package, along with the nutritional percent per serving of the contents. This information can be useful in ensuring basic nutrition from your food stocks.

Remember that people have and do live on far fewer calories and very unbalanced diets for a long time. Under emergency conditions the ideal 2,000 calories may have to be reduced and ideal requirements and limitations put aside temporarily, but serious health issues will develop if a diet of less than 2,000 calories is sustained for more than a few weeks. Fat, cholesterol, salt, and sugar limitations should not stop you from eating when you need calories, protein, minerals, and vitamins to stay alive and healthy. The list below is a good start for a home "survival pantry." These foods are economical, store easily, and have a long shelf life. They are best if vacuum-packed and kept at moderate temperatures. To ensure proper rotation, mark the storage date on each container. Since there really is no maximum amount of food to store, I have included a suggested minimum per person per year as a goal. I found wide differences in shelf-life estimates. The ones shown below are averages of several sources, but in all cases the use of vacuum-packaging and cool dry storage will prolong shelf life.

- **Pasta:** Spaghetti, macaroni, and other noodles are high in carbohydrates and easy to use in lots of dishes. Pasta has a shelf life of at least fifteen years. Minimum per person: twenty-five pounds.
- **Rice**: High in carbohydrates and useful in many dishes. Store only whole grain rice, as instant rice will not keep well. Minimum per person: twenty-five pounds.
- **Legumes**: Pinto beans, black beans, garbanzo beans, red beans, lentils, and other types store for twenty to thirty years, are easy to cook, and provide a good source of protein. Minimum per person: thirty pounds.
- **Grits:** Grits are made from the cornmealing process and are a good source of nutrition. They can be used as cereal, fried, or in many recipes. You can use them to replace part or all of the recommended grain stores.
- **Nuts**: Usually vacuum-packed, these store for decades and are a great source of protein and other nutrients. Minimum per person: ten pounds.
- **Peanut butter:** Seriously? A forty-ounce jar of peanut butter contains 6,650 calories. That's more than a three-day food supply. But it has a shelf life of about three to four years, so you need to rotate it. Minimum per person: three jars.
- **Whole grains:** Whole grains are often sold as survival foods. They do provide good nutrition, but to make baked goods (e.g., bread), you need a grain mill to grind the grain into flour. Whole grains keep much longer than flour. Oats can be made into oatmeal or used in baking. Minimum per person: twenty-five pounds.
- **Dried fruits:** Dried fruits—such as dates, raisins, apples, bananas, figs, and apricots—store for many years and provide important vitamins. Minimum per person: ten pounds.
- **Meat jerky:** Jerky or dehydrated meat is an important source of calories and protein for your diet. If you make jerky yourself, be sure to salt it and remove all the fat before drying. Vacuum-packed jerky should keep for at least two years and can be reconstituted in soups or stews or eaten as is.
- **Powdered milk:** Powdered milk is a good source of vitamins and other nutrients. Store-bought product should be immediately vacuum-packed for the best shelf life, but the vitamins degrade over time. Powdered milk specifically packaged in cans for storage will last up to fifteen years, but should be repackaged in airtight containers once opened. Minimum per person: five pounds.
- **Powdered eggs:** These are nutritious and have a shelf life of about ten years if kept in airtight or vacuum-packed containers. They can be used as scrambled eggs or in a variety of recipes. Minimum per person: five pounds.
- **Canned vegetables:** Canned vegetables (e.g., spinach, corn, green beans, and carrots) are essential to health and keep for four years or longer. Vegetables can be stored for many years, but canned fruits

should be rotated every few years, as the acid can eat through the cans over time.* Minimum per person: fifteen to twenty cans.

- **Canned meats**: Canned meats (e.g., Spam, corned beef, or Vienna sausage) are very nutritious and store well. You can also stock up on canned tuna and chicken for variety. The recommended shelf life is two to four years, but I have used products that were as much as fifteen years old. Canned anchovies and sardines in oil keep indefinitely. Minimum per person: twelve cans.
- **Bouillon and soup mixes**: Bouillon cubes and soup mix envelopes take up very little space and provide a way to create tasty soups from what you have stored and what you may be able to gather. I carry bouillon cubes in my survival packs so I can make frog, worm, and weed stew taste like chicken!
- **Honey**: Sometimes called the perfect food, honey really keeps indefinitely and can substitute for sugar in many uses. Minimum per person: two to three pounds.
- **Sugar**: Sugar is a nonperishable staple if kept in airtight and dry containers. It can be used in all kinds of recipes. I recommend keeping both white and brown sugar. Minimum per person: five pounds.
- **Flour**: Useful in all kinds of cooking and baking, flour can last up to ten years if sealed and dry. Minimum per person: fifty pounds.
- **Coffee and tea**: Depending on your taste, these beverages offer comfort, warmth, and stimulation under any conditions, and are great trade goods. Minimum per person: ten pounds of coffee or four hundred tea bags.
- **Vinegar**: Vinegar has many uses in cooking, food preservation, cleaning, and even alternative medicine. You definitely want to have a few gallons.
- **Cooking oils and shortening**: A necessary ingredient in baking and frying. Minimum per person: one gallon.
- **Salt**: Used to enhance flavors and as a preservative. It will be in big demand during a prolonged emergency. Minimum per person: five pounds.
- **Spices**: A good selection of spices can make otherwise bland "survival food" more enjoyable. The selection depends on your taste.
- **Other stuff**: There are lots of other options and additions. You can add freeze-dried meals to reduce storage space, stock spaghetti sauce to enhance the pastas, substitute molasses for some of the honey, or exchange Bisquick (shelf life: two to three years) baking mix for flour. Maybe add some cans of baked beans or some of your own canned foods. You may throw in some hard candy, which lasts a long time if kept dry and cool, for comfort and quick energy.

**Based on examination of a twenty-five-year food stock opened in 1995.

The bottom line on food: Don't waste too much time fretting about where to start. Just start buying and storing any of the items below.

A number of options for food pantry (left to right): homemade food stock consisting of pasta, rice, beans, oatmeal, and other storable foods in vacuum-packed bags; stack of three ready-made, thirty-day containers of freeze-dried meals; box of six number-ten cans of survival foods from a preparedness supply outlet; and tote bins full of freeze-dried foods, MREs, and canned goods.

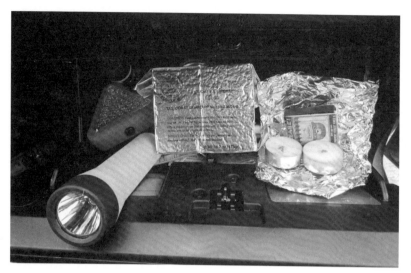

Remember, it's not what you have but what you have with you that counts. The concentrated life-boat ration food bars in this glove compartment (center) provide 2,000 calories to get you through a short-term situation, and store indefinitely under hot and cold conditions. Note also the tea candles and aluminum foil for staying warm in a vehicle caught in a storm, and the flashlight and emergency flasher on the left.

2. GROWING YOUR OWN FOOD

Gardening is a healthy hobby that can provide extra food to meet emergency needs. Since plants take months to grow and bear edible vegetables, you should have an established garden system going before you need it. You will also want to stock up on seeds for future gardening. Most commercial seeds are hybrids that rapidly decline in fertility. The seeds from the resulting plants may not be viable at all for future crops.

Vacuum-packaged, nonhybrid, non-GMO seeds that have a shelf life of at least five to ten years or longer are available from preparedness supply outlets. Stocking up on these can give you a guarantee of long-term regenerative production. If you have lots of room, "farm-style" plow-and-furrow gardening can work, but raised-bed, intensive gardening produces more vegetables in less space while reducing weeds. Since you have no need for walkways between rows, you can plant closer together and do the tending from outside the beds. The beds are usually three to four feet square and about twelve inches high with an eighteen- to twenty-four-inch walkway around them. The small size of the beds also allows for rigging plastic covers over the seedlings for early planting and for netting to protect from birds and animals. Keep in mind that the average American consumes about 985,500 calories per year! Unless you have several acres per person, possess good soil, can store everything you grow, and can fend off insects and pests, your garden is going to be supplemental or subsistence at best. But it will still be an important part of your food supply system. If you are not going to can produce, such root vegetables as potatoes, carrots, and beets are good survival foods. They keep in cool, dry storage or in the ground for a long time after the growing season.

Indoor gardening methods have advanced considerably in recent years. These are ideal for providing fresh vegetables in the off seasons or

A small raised-bed, intensive garden like this one can provide significant additions to your food supplies. Focus on growing vegetables that can be stored, canned, or dried. iStock/Christina Jaramillo.

in apartments and condominiums. One drawback is that you need to either take up window space or use grow lights. Potted vegetable plants have now been supplanted by stackable and self-watering systems. More advanced hydroponic and aquaponic systems are also on the market. Hydroponic systems grow plants in soil-free trays, where the plants are nourished from chemical nutrients flowing below them. These systems require the use of special liquid nutrients. Aquaponic systems grow plants the same way, but no artificial nutrients are needed. Fish are raised in adjoining tanks and the fish waste product provides nutrients for the plants. At the same time, the plant material is used as fish food. Both the fish and the vegetables are harvested for human consumption. Maintaining a balanced closed-cycle system can provide a steady supply of food in a relatively small space, such as a shed, garage, or basement.

Above: Indoor, self-watering, staked systems like this can provide year-round food in a small space.

A small aquaponic system shown at a survival exposition. When in use, there would be fish living in the lower tank. The fish fertilize the plants while the plants provide the fish with food. No outside chemicals are necessary. You balance the system by harvesting fish or vegetables as needed.

3. FORAGING

Once the local supermarkets are cleaned out and any stored food is depleted, you will need to forage for food. Any foodstuffs that are not in the possession of others is fair game for foraging in desperate situations. Edible corn, soybeans, and other crops may be available. Nuts from trees, wild berries, and a wide variety of edible "weeds" can be a lifesaving supplement to your diet. Wild edible plants are plentiful in most regions and will not be depleted as fast as crops, fish, and game because most people do not know how to recognize what and what not to eat.

In a survival situation you need nourishment but cannot afford to become ill, so pass on any plant that seems questionable. I would not eat any kind of mushrooms, period. It may be better to spend a few hours testing available plants for edibility than spending time and energy searching for known edibles. Don't wait until you are out of food and hungry to start foraging for edibles. A rapid shift from prepared food to wild edibles (even safe ones) will result in cramps, nausea, and diarrhea. These conditions result in the loss of nutrition and in dehydration. Consider having salt, bouillon cubes, and other seasoning in your survival pantry to make these unfamiliar plants more appetizing.

Here is the standard way to safely test for the edibility of a plant:

- Rub a small amount of the plant juice from leaves or roots on the back of your hand. Watch for irritation or rash developing in about thirty minutes.
- Chew a small quantity and spit it out. Do not swallow any! Monitor for ill effects during the next hour.
- Chew and swallow a very small amount. If unsafe, you will feel ill in the next four to six hours.
- Repeat the process.
- If there are still no ill effects, you can assume the plant is safe to eat.
- If there is any indication of poisoning, induce vomiting immediately.
- Spend some time looking for these plants in your local area. You are sure to find some of them. Try them in a salad or cooked.

The following are just a few common edible plants. I selected these because they are likely to be found in any vacant lot, backyard or woodland area. Unfortunately, the cattail, bulrush, and arrowhead have been replaced by several invasive species in some areas.

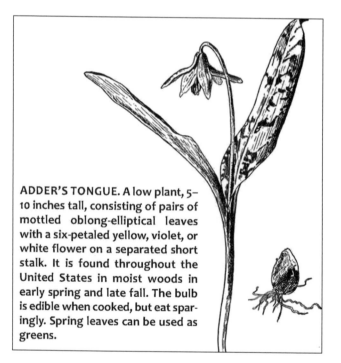

ADDER'S TONGUE. A low plant, 5–10 inches tall, consisting of pairs of mottled oblong-elliptical leaves with a six-petaled yellow, violet, or white flower on a separated short stalk. It is found throughout the United States in moist woods in early spring and late fall. The bulb is edible when cooked, but eat sparingly. Spring leaves can be used as greens.

Arrowhead. A small plant found throughout the United States in wet ground and shallow water. Arrow-shaped leaves appear at the end of individual stems. Flowers appear on separated stems. Boiled or baked bulbs taste like potatoes. Follow the threadlike root down to find the bulb.

Bulrush. A small, marsh grass–like plant consisting of a long stem with small seeds at the upper end. Light green in color, it is found in slow streams, marshes, and at the edge of lakes. The base of the stalk and young shoots are edible raw or cooked. Young roots are edible. Roots may be dried and pounded into flour.

Burdbock. A large plant that may grow as high as nine feet but averages somewhat less. It has coarse leaves and purplish flowers compressed in a burr-like head. It is found throughout the northern United States in open wastelands, along roadsides, and along streams. Tender stalks can be peeled and eaten raw or cooked. Roots may also be cleaned and cooked. Use two changes of water when cooking it.

Cattail. This survival food classic has tall stalks with flat leaves. Its average height is about four feet but may reach over six feet. Flowers appear at top of stalks. After the flower, a dense brown spike remains. Found year-round throughout the United States in wet and swampy areas. The leaves lie down in winter, but the bulbous spike remains. Roots may be roasted, boiled, dried and pounded into flour, or cooked to form a thick soup. Chew out the starch. Young shoots may be eaten. Young spikes are edible raw or cooked before they flower.

Chicory. Light-blue flowers grow close along stiff branching stems averaging three feet high. Flowers wither rapidly in direct sun. Chicory is found throughout most of the United States along roadsides, in pastures, and in wastelands. Dried roots make a good coffee substitute. Young spring greens boiled in two changes of water resemble spinach.

Ground nut. Found throughout most of the eastern United States in low, damp soil. This is a smooth, slender climbing vine with milky juice, growing five to ten feet in length. The root system consists of a number of tubers connected by fibrous strands. The leaves are compound with five to eight oval oval leaflets. Flowers are brownish purple with pods resembling beans. One of the best wild foods, its tubers may be eaten raw, boiled, or roasted.

Dandelion. This green is found worldwide. Roots may be eaten raw. Cook the leaves as you would spinach. Make a tea by boiling the leaves for a good cold remedy.

Fireweed. Found throughout the northern and western United States, it often grows in burned-out areas (hence "fireweed"), open woods, and along roads. It is a tall plant, growing from two to six feet high, with purple and pink flowers. Young shoots and leaves are good raw or cooked. Add salt if possible.

Curly Dock. A tall plant growing from two to four feet tall, it is found throughout the United States in cultivated or waste ground. It has deep taproots and many smooth marginal leaves with long-stemmed, small greenish flowers that fade to a reddish brown. Tender leaves may be cooked. Parboil to remove a slight bitter taste. Seeds can be ground to make a cake or gruel.

Purslane. This is a low ground plant often found growing from cracks in rocks or sidewalks, in fields, and along streams. The leaves are juicy, soft, and oval in shape. They are normally light green but may have a red tinge. The flowers are small and yellow, and have five petals. Leaves and stems may be eaten raw and, although a bit sour, are a good source of water. Leaves and stems may also be steamed and eaten like spinach.

Pokeweed. This is a tall plant from four to eight feet high. The young, pale green leaves come up in bunches at the base of last year's stalks. Mature plants have red stems. The flowers are small, grow in clusters, and may be tinged with purple. Dark blue berries follow the flowers. Pokeweed is common throughout the United States in fallow fields, forest clearings, and along roads. Caution: Roots and berries are poisonous. Cut stems well above ground level when they are four to six inches high. Boil, rinse, and boil again. Use as an asparagus substitute.

Plantain. Long spear-shaped leaves spring from the ground on a rather coarse stem. Small flowers grow compacted on a separated stalk. It is found throughout the northeastern and north central United States in lawns, fields, and woods. Boil early shoots as greens.

Shepherd's Purse. Found throughout most of the United States in fields and wastelands, this plant grows to a height of about ten inches. The leaves are pear shaped, and the lower leaves are deeply and irregularly lobed. Flowers are small and white. Young leaves can be eaten raw and taste a bit like cabbage.

Thistle. This plant is found throughout most of the United States in pastures and roadsides. It may consist of one or two stalks, growing from one to four feet high, from dark green or silver green. Flowers may be pink, white, purple, or yellow. Remove young plant stalks and leaves. Peel and boil stems until tender.

Solomon's Seal. Found throughout most of the United States in moist areas and along streams, Solomon's seal has a slender stalk with lacy-shaped or ovate leaves growing alternately. Flowers grow singly or in twos or threes from the leaf axle and are light green turning into dark blue berries. The fleshy roots may be boiled or roasted and eaten like parsnips. The young shoots are also edible.

Watercress. This is found throughout most of the United States where running streams exist. The flowers are white and usually grow in clusters. The leaves are dark green and somewhat rounded. Leaves can be eaten raw or added to other greens for flavor. Caution: Take care when picking watercress since the deadly water hemlock usually grows in similar places. Do not use watercress from polluted streams.

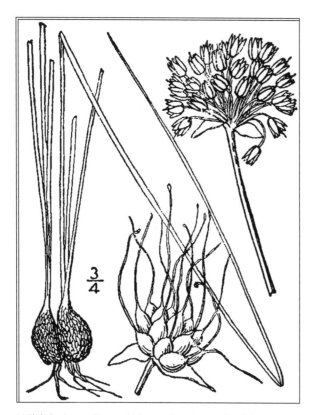

Wild Onions. Found throughout most of the United States, these look and taste similar to the domestic onion. Long, grasslike, flat, juicy leaves originate from the ground surface. Leaves will have a strong onion smell. Use the same way as you do domestic onions. Cooked syrup is good for colds.

Clover. The blossoms, stems, and seeds are all edible. Clean and dip in salted water if possible. It is found throughout the United States in fields and open lands.

4. FISHING

I once met a fellow who refused to learn other survival skills because he insisted that if you could fish you could always survive. While I would not go that far, I must admit that the ability to catch fish could be an essential lifesaving skill in many situations. With the exception of the desert and high mountains, most areas of the United States are well supplied with rivers, streams, lakes, and oceanfronts teeming with a wide variety of fish. In a sustained survival situation, the ability to catch these sources of nutrition could be critical. Fishing takes less energy and materials than hunting and trapping, and fish flesh is well suited to salting, smoking, and drying for preservation. As any angler will attest, fishing is tricky and not always successful, but this is "sports fishing," where rules apply and it is not a life-or-death situation. You would be well advised to stock up on fishing equipment now, even if fishing is not your hobby. Be aware that a lot of people fish, and once food supplies get low, the area lakes and streams may well be fished out in a short time.

Fishing Tips

- If fishing near the shore, early morning and early evening are the best times.
- In deep (offshore) waters, anytime is good for fishing.
- Some say that fishing is often good just before a storm.
- Watch for fish jumping at bugs to identify a good spot.

- The best fishing spots may be:
  - At the edge of weed beds
  - Under fallen logs
  - Areas full of lily pads and other plants
  - At the base of rapids
  - Under overhanging rocks and banks

Fishing Methods and Devices

While traditional line and pole fishing may be effective, a survival situation may demand faster and more reliable methods. You may need to build shelters, forage, hunt, trap, and even fight, so sitting on the bank for hours may not be an option. If you do not have any traditional fishing items (e.g., line, hooks, poles), you can certainly improvise what you need. The following illustrations provide some methods you can use. Studying them and trying them can help you establish a reliable food supply method for most survival situations. In an urban situation or a general collapse scenario, someone who can catch, supply, and preserve fish from regional sources will be able to trade and barter well.

Tidal Fishing

When I was in Hawaii, I met natives who were using simple stone fish traps to catch fish every day. This was a simple stone square with the open end facing toward shore in shallow water. When the tide goes out, the fish are left trapped. The natives just go out and net them to feed their families and sell to local markets.

Survival Fishing Kits

Fishing kits are usually included in military survival kits. Such kits take up very little room and have the potential of providing a reliable supply of food with a minimum of effort.

- Twenty to thirty feet of twenty-pound-test fishing line, also usable for snares and other applications
- Assorted hooks and sinkers
- Assorted lures and dehydrated bait (optional)
- Poles and bobbers (can usually be improvised from available materials)

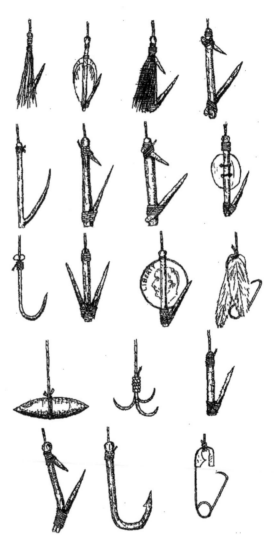

Above are just a few ways to improvise fishing hooks and lures using pins, wire, bone, wood, and even stone chips. You can use worms, grubs, insects, and other items for bait.

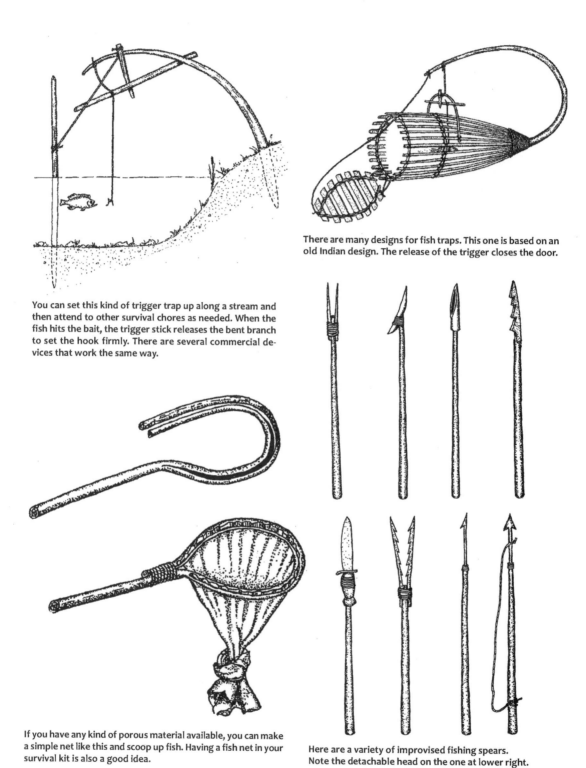

There are many designs for fish traps. This one is based on an old Indian design. The release of the trigger closes the door.

You can set this kind of trigger trap up along a stream and then attend to other survival chores as needed. When the fish hits the bait, the trigger stick releases the bent branch to set the hook firmly. There are several commercial devices that work the same way.

If you have any kind of porous material available, you can make a simple net like this and scoop up fish. Having a fish net in your survival kit is also a good idea.

Here are a variety of improvised fishing spears. Note the detachable head on the one at lower right.

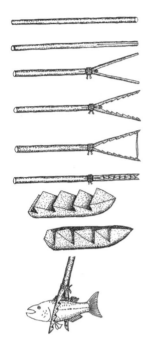

For some types of fishing, trigger sticks are even better than spears. Start with a green pole about 5.5 feet long and 1.5 inches in diameter. Split carefully about eighteen inches up. Tie off to keep the split from growing and then spread the two sides. Cut the teeth as shown. Insert the trigger stick so it holds the jaws open but will trip away on impact with the fish. Be sure to store the trigger stick closed.

Note: when using a spear or a trigger stick, be aware that water distorts the location of the fish a bit. Practice will help you compensate for this.

Gigging is a method of fishing where a device with multiple gigs, or points, is dangled in the water. when a fish goes to the bait on the shaft, the device is yanked upward, thus gigging the fish.

Simple tidal fish trap made from volcanic rocks on the Kona Coast.

Hawaiian fisherman readies his net.

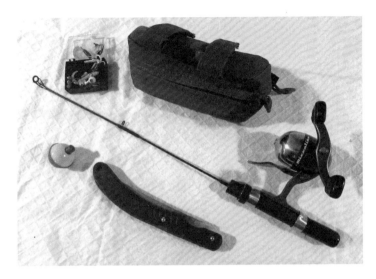

This small survival fishing kit fits in the pack, but netting, trapping, and spearing are all justified in a survival situation.

Acts of Desperation

There are some drastic methods of catching fish that would only be justified as a last resort. They are illegal and irresponsible, but if you are starving, these methods could provide a number of fish in a short time. The downside is that they may deplete the stock of fish you will need for the long term.

Using explosives to shock the fish to the surface is pretty drastic and may attract unwanted attention. The fish that float to the surface are easy to net or spear until they recover.

Rotenone is a commercial pesticide available at many garden centers. It is made from the same plants used by natives to poison fish for centuries. This product is very toxic to fish and insects but only slightly toxic to humans. Used in smaller lakes and ponds, it can result in a lot of dead but edible fish. It won't be much good if used in flowing water or larger rivers and lakes.

5. TRAPPING

Trapping takes less effort than hunting and fishing, and can be done without weapons or complicated gear. It is also quiet and effective. Use the same methods of finding the best areas for game as apply to hunting and set your traps in game trails, near water, and where signs of game are evident. Trapping may well be illegal in your area, but certainly it is justified under survival conditions. Although the trap systems illustrated can be enlarged to catch big game, such as deer, you have to consider the hazard that you may accidently catch, injure, or kill a human being in them. Below are several easy-to-make designs for animal and bird traps. You can use flexible wire or strong cordage in construction.

The deadfall trap uses gravity and a falling object to disable or kill the prey. It is a bit tricky to set up but is effective.

This detail of the trigger system for a deadfall illustrates the use of notches.

Another noose and bent-sapling system with a very simple trigger system.

This square knot trap is good for catching birds and small game. Instead of a trigger and spring, the trapper waits in hiding and pulls hard on the line when the prey enters the noose.

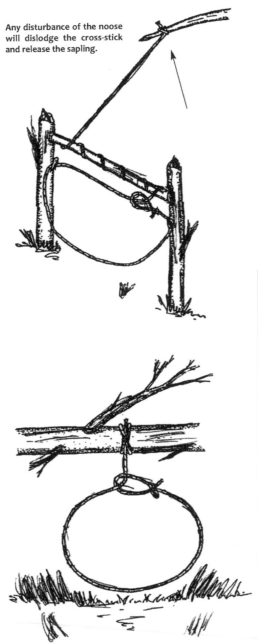

Any disturbance of the noose will dislodge the cross-stick and release the sapling.

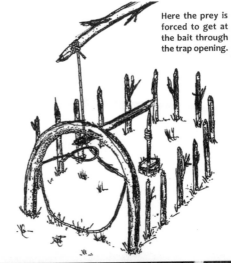

Here the prey is forced to get at the bait through the trap opening.

This very simple noose trap can be set up on a game trail or baited. It is very effective for catching squirrels.

This classic trap uses the spring action of a bent sapling to close the noose. It can be baited or set near a game trail. Note the hook and notch trigger system.

Any disturbance of the noose will dislodge the cross-stick and release the sapling.

This very simple noose trap can be set up on a game trail or baited. It is very effective for catching squirrels.

Here, the prey is forced to get at the bait through the trap opening.

This classic trap uses the spring action of a bent sapling to close the noose. It can be baited or set near a game trail. Note the hook and notch trigger system.

6. HUNTING

Like fishing, hunting is an art acquired by practice. If you are not a hunter and need to hunt for food in an emergency, you will have significant challenges. Assuming that the emergency has affected the general population, the woods will be full of both experienced and inexperienced hunters. Your chances of getting shot may be better than your chances of getting game. Within a few weeks, most of the game will have either been killed or scared off into the deep woods. Hunting and preserving game in advance will certainly help build up your survival food supplies. If you are in a wilderness or refuge survival situation, hunting may be a practical option. I usually have a .22-caliber rifle, compact survival bow, and a slingshot in my survival pack. This gives me a number of quiet options for taking small game and birds.

Today's big and small game are the surviving descendants of millions of years of being hunted. Their senses are keen, and they are aware of any scent, sound, or sign of your approach. Here are a few general tips for hunting.

- Remember that game have the same survival needs as you do. Hunt where they will find food, water, and shelter.
- Most game is more active during the early morning and early evening before and just after sunset.
- Watch for game trails and tracks. Game usually wears a path toward water. Semi-cleared routes and trampled ground indicate the best places to hunt.
- Approach game from downwind to avoid them getting your scent.
- Be absolutely quiet even if you do not see game in the area. If you are talking, crunching on twigs, or rustling brush, they will be gone before you see them.
- Look for broken branches, droppings, and urine as signs of animal activity.
- Use binoculars or a good scope on your rifle or crossbow to extend your range.

Above are some tracks of game you may be hunting in a survival situation.

7. CANNING

Basic Canning Procedure

Fruits and vegetables need to be prepared before canning. All produce should be washed and cut into pieces to fit into the containers. Such fruits as pears and peaches can be canned whole but pitted if necessary. Dipping them in ascorbic acid or packing them in sugar syrup will help to preserve flavor and color. To raw-pack items, just closely pack the cut vegetables or fruit into the jars and pour in boiling water or syrup, leaving about a half inch of headroom at the top of the jar. For hot-pack canning, the vegetable or fruit should be thoroughly steamed or boiled in water, juices, or syrup, and then quickly poured into the containers. The two primary canning methods are pressure cooker and boiling-water bath.

Boiling-water-bath canning is the best method for acidic fruits, including tomatoes. Vegetables that have already been pickled (e.g., beets, cucumbers) can be canned by this method as well. The basic steps in boiling-water-bath canning are as follows:

- Fill the canner pot half full of hot water and then lower the basket of closed, food-filled jars into the water.
- Add boiling water to about two inches above the tops of the jars.
- Cover the canner pot and bring the water to a boil.
- Reduce heat to maintain a rapid boil but not a boil-over, and add more boiling water (from a kettle) as needed to maintain levels.
- When the time is up (see table below), use tongs to remove the jars immediately.
- Tighten lids if needed, wearing gloves to avoid burns, and set out on a rack to cool.

The boiling-water-bath times are for quart containers. The time for pints is usually five minutes less.

PRODUCT	PACKED RAW	PACKED COOKED/HOT
Tomatoes	40 minutes	35 minutes
Sauerkraut	20 minutes	20 minutes
Apples	20 minutes	20 minutes
Berries	15 minutes	15 minutes
Peaches	30 minutes	25 minutes
Pears	30 minutes	25 minutes

The pressure-cooker method is used for canning non-acidic vegetables. The steps for this method are outlined below.

1. Pour two to three inches of boiling water into the bottom of the pressure cooker.
2. Place the closed jars on a rack at the bottom of the pressure cooker, making sure that the jars do not touch each other.
3. Fasten the lid on the pressure cooker and turn the flame up to maximum.
4. Let the steam exhaust for ten minutes.
5. When the steam coming out of the vent just above the opening is nearly invisible, close the vent.
6. When the pressure reaches about eight pounds, lower the flame a bit.
7. When the pressure reaches ten pounds, start timing to hold the pressure required for the specific vegetable and container size (see table on the following page).
8. When the time is up, remove the pressure cooker from the heat and let it cool naturally.
9. When the pressure reaches zero, open the vent, remove the cover, and remove the jars.
10. Place jars on rack to cool, with space between them. Tighten jar covers as needed.

The time for pints is about five minutes less than for boiling-water bath, except corn, which is still fifty-five minutes.

PRODUCT	TIME TO MAINTAIN TEN POUNDS OF PRESSURE FOR QUARTS
Corn	55 minutes
Potatoes	40 minutes
Beets	35 minutes
Beans	25 minutes
Carrots	30 minutes
Lima Beans	50 minutes
Peas	40 minutes

8. DRYING AND FREEZE-DRYING

Drying is one of the oldest methods of food preservation. Most vegetables, fruits, and meats can be dried. Drying can be accomplished using heat from a campfire, a stove, or a purpose-built dryer. The three elements of drying are as follows:

1. Cutting the food into very thin pieces, usually about a quarter-inch thick to ensure full drying.
2. Drying at temperatures of between 120 and 150 degrees Fahrenheit over an extended time. Dry it; don't burn it.
3. Ensuring a good airflow on all surfaces by using a rack screen or by turning it frequently.

The following steps are for pretreating and preparing food for drying:

- Remove all peel, seeds, pits, and husks from vegetables and fruits.
- Remove all bone, blood, and excess fat from meats before drying.
- Remove all blood and bones and thoroughly clean fish. Then steam or bake till flaky before drying.
- Steam or roast meats and poultry to 165 degrees before drying.
- You can soak cut fruits in lemon juice or ascorbic acid solution before drying.
- Blanching can ensure safe drying without destroying nutrients. This can be accomplished by placing the cut foods in a covered pot of boiling water for three minutes before placing them in the dryer or by placement in the steaming tray of a steamer for three to five minutes.

The following are recommended drying time and temperatures:

- Meat and poultry: 145 to 155 degrees for four to seven hours
- Vegetables: 125 to 135 degrees for ten to twelve hours
- Fruits: 135 to 145 degrees for twenty-four to thirty-six hours
- Juicy vegetables, such as tomatoes (really a fruit): ten to eighteen hours
- Juicy fruits, such as peaches and nectarines: up to forty-eight hours

Some food dryers, like this one, cost about one hundred dollars. Homesized freeze-drying units like this one can be expensive, but have a reliable power supply, they can do a great job of drying freeze-dried and vacuum-packed foods last for decades and save various vegetables and fruits. You can also make jerky in them.

Home-sized freeze-drying units like this one can be expensive, but freeze-dried and vacuum-packed foods last for decades and save space and weight.

Amish drying house with small stove in the center and racks for food on each side. The Amish dry, can, and cure all their foods without benefit of electricity.

9. SALTING, CURING, AND PICKLING

These methods are more complicated than just dumping salt or vinegar on foods. Salt draws the moisture out of meat and fish, thereby making them more resistant to fungus and bacteria. The acid content of vinegar in pickling accomplishes the same thing. A brief description of a few generic processes is provided here, but the reader should seek more specific instructions and recipes for various foods. Note that both dry-salting and brining methods require the use of cylindrical crockery containers, cheesecloth, and a lot of salt. Keeping salt and vinegar in bulk quantities is recommended for survival stockpiling, as they are valuable for food preservation, trade goods, and other applications.

Basic Dry-Salting Procedure

- Blanch vegetables by steaming over boiling water for three to five minutes. Then plunge into cold water.
- Fill a crock with alternating one-inch layers of vegetables and enough salt to completely cover each layer. You should be using about one pound of salt for every four pounds of vegetables.
- Leave about four to five inches of space above the last layer of salt.
- Cover the top with cheesecloth so it overlaps the sides by several inches after weighing down the center with a plate to form space about four to five inches deep.
- After twenty-four hours, juices should come up through the cheesecloth into the space. If this does not happen, add a solution of three teaspoons of salt and one cup of water to cover.
- Store the crock in a cool location and use food as needed.
- You will need to soak and drain salted vegetables several times to reduce salt content before cooking.

Basic Brining

- Food should be blanched, as for dry-salting, and then placed into a crock (one to five gallons).
- Make a brine solution of one pound of salt to one gallon of water. You will need one gallon of brine for every two gallons of vegetables.
- Leave about four to five inches above the last layer of vegetables.
- Cover the top with cheesecloth so it overlaps the sides by several inches after weighing down the center with a plate or plates to keep the vegetables submerged and to form a four- to five-inch space.
- The next day add about one half pound of salt on top for every five pounds of vegetables and then about an eighth of a pound of salt for every five pounds of vegetables each week thereafter.
- Skim off any scum that rises and wait four to eight weeks until no more bubbles rise to the top. Then store in a cool location.
- You will need to soak and drain salted vegetables several times to reduce salt content before cooking.

Basic Pickling Solution

A solution of 2.75 cups of vinegar and one quarter cup of salt (non-iodized) to three cups of water for every four pounds of vegetables to be pickled. The vinegar should be at 5 percent acidity level. Apple vinegar gives a good flavor, but other types work as well.

Basic Pickling Procedure

- Thoroughly clean the vegetables.
- Place vegetables in sterilized glass jars.

- Add the pickling solution to cover vegetable and fill the jar. Note that you can add spices and sugar to improve flavors depending on the vegetable (e.g., dill, cinnamon, cloves)
- Seal the jar and shake vigorously.
- The shelf life of properly pickled produce can be over five years if kept closed and in a cool environment.

10. FOOD FOR SURVIVAL PACKS

The content of bug-out bags is addressed elsewhere in this book, but some quantity of food must be a part of any survival kit and pack. The main considerations involved in the selection are (1) how long you will be dependent on the packed food; and (2) how much you can carry under the anticipated condition. (See Chapter 5, "Ten Things You Should Have in Your Survival Pack.")

Compact survival kits:

These may be carried or stored in your vehicle for short-term emergencies while stranded outdoors. The primary need here is high-calorie food that keeps long term, needs no cooking, and takes up little space.

Recommended food contents: Depending on the size of the kit, energy bars, granola, and trail snacks are good choices but should be rotated at least annually. For long-term storage and maximum nutrition, you should consider US Coast Guard Lifeboat Rations. These 16.7-ounce, 4x3.5x2-inch packages contain six food bars totaling 2,400 calories and store for at least five years under any conditions.

Evacuation packs or bug-out bags

These are intended for carrying on foot for several days until you reach help. Here you need three to four days of lightweight food supplies that can be eaten as is or cooked. Space and weight are important considerations.

Recommended food contents: If you have included a small Sterno or other stove, you can include a variety of dehydrated camp meals, but I still recommend the Lifeboat Rations mentioned above or energy bars since there is no guarantee that you will be able to stop and cook. Remember that you need to pack 2,000 calories per day or more per person.

Survival packs:

These full-sized camping packs are intended to provide all the survival necessities for at least seven days. Such packs include stoves and fire starters, so foods that require cooking and dehydrating are practical and necessary.

Recommended food contents: You are not going to be able to carry seven or more days of non-dehydrated foods, but you can carry nuts, jerky, dried fruit, pasta, and rice. The most efficient (i.e., small, light) meals are dehydrated camping meals. You should have at least two days of no-cook foods for traveling. Since you have to pack shelter, clothing, stove, weapons, water filters, and everything else you need and carry it for some distance, calories per pound is the most important criterion.

Maximizing Freezer Time

In a long-term power outage, you are going to want to use all that food in your freezer before you start depleting your survival foods. Of course, if it's winter and outside temperatures are consistently below freezing, you can just put all that frozen food into closed containers and place it outside. You can have tote bins in an unheated shed or on a closed porch. If you are going to put the food outside, you must use sealed metal containers and place them in a shady area to keep animals out and prevent sunlight warming from the container. Large military ammunition boxes are ideal for this. The following information from government studies should help you preserve the food in the freezer for a while longer:

- Foods in full or nearly full freezers during a power outage may stay good for two to four days without power. For this reason you should keep bags of ice as filler when the freezer is less than full.
- Food stored in a freezer that is half full or less may be good for one to two days without power.
- Stored meat will stay cold longer than a mix of foods, so keep one freezer primarily for meat and another for the rest of the food, if you can.
- The colder the room, the longer the refrigerator will stay cold, so the freezer should be in a cool, unheated basement or garage if possible.
- Containers of frozen water or any ice can help maintain a full freezer's temperatures close to four days. For this to be effective, you must think and act ahead since ice may be hard to get and impossible to make after power is lost.
- Prefilled milk jugs or soda containers partially full with water (ice expands about 10 percent) must be kept beside the freezer. When there is notable space open in the freezer, insert prefilled water containers and let freeze.
- The hard part is getting into the habit of keeping water-filled containers beside the freezer (they do take up space) and actually adding them to the freezer each time. Of course, these jugs are also part of your reserve water supply.

Covering the freezer with layers of Styrofoam or urethane boards to provide another layer of insulation on all surfaces (except the heat-exchanging coils) can add more days to food preservation inside. It can also save energy usage when the power is on. If a foam board layer is used over the heat-exchanging coils, the freezer should be unplugged to prevent damaging the freezer should the power return before the cap is removed.

- One inch of Styrofoam board (usually R5) drops the energy used by half and then drops the energy use by 50 percent. It will also reduce the transfer of heat by 80 percent.
- To reduce the remaining heat transfer by another 80 percent (a total reduction of 96 percent), apply another two inches of Styrofoam board, for a total of three inches, or 1.5 inches of urethane foam. These foam boards can be permanently attached to improve energy efficiency so long as the heat-exchanging coils are left uncovered.
- To reduce the remaining 4 percent transfer of heat to 0.8 percent requires four *additional* inches and is really at the point of uneconomical diminishing returns.

CHAPTER 11
Ten Ways to Start and Maintain a Fire

Being able to start a fire is considered a prime survival skill. I have seen folks use up a whole pack of matches trying to get a fire going under fairly good conditions. I have also seen good fires go out because of poor fire tending. Successful, first-time conversion of spark to fire is critical, especially if your spark source (e.g., matches, flint) is limited. Patience and preparation are the keys to success. The following are a few of the most common fire craft techniques.

1. FIRE BY MATCHES AND STRIKERS

There are many complicated methods for starting a fire, but none is as simple or efficient as just striking a match. Close behind matches in efficiency are the various "metal match" magnesium fire-starting devices marketed to campers. These are a much more effective spark-generating system than flint and steel, but still require the same careful techniques to get you from the spark to a flame. Waterproof camp matches and "metal match" devices are reliable and easy-to-use fire-starting systems. I recommend that you carry either of these devices in every jacket and vest. All other methods, including flint and steel, should be considered alternatives.

Starting a fire with a large magnesium fire starter

Note also the magnifying glass. Such devices were a must before the invention of the match. Left front is a pocket-sized magnesium spark-striking device. I recommend one of these in every jacket pocket and survival kit. At center is a pack of common camping matches. These are waterproof, but I keep them in a plastic bag anyway. The larger magnesium striker on the right provides a big reliable spark, a must for the full-sized backpack or bug-out bag.

A Cheap and Reliable Fire Starter

To ignite the flame on welding torches, welders use strikers. These very simple devices consist of a spring wire handle with a small metal cup on the end. One end of the handle holds the cup, while the other end is threaded to hold a small flint mounted on threaded nipples. There is rough grit in the cup that lies against the flint. Squeezing the handle moves the flint across the grit to generate a good spark. The cup catches a bit of the welding gas so that ignition is ensured. To use as a survival fire starter, you place lint, cotton, very dry grass, or other tinder in the cup and just squeeze the handle. The cup holds the starter near to the spark and protects it from the wind. Strikers are cheap (a few dollars each) and replacement flints are even cheaper. This reliable fire starter weighs only about two ounces, is available wherever welding supplies are sold, and is better than the more expensive commercial fire starters. *Caution:* If you carry one in your pack, be sure to open it up so the flint cannot accidentally get pushed across the grit and start a fire that you do not want in your pack.

2. FIRE BY FLINT AND STEEL

Starting a fire with flint and steel takes a bit of practice. You are better off with matches or a magnesium device. However, the skills required could allow you to create a spark using flint or other hard metals and rocks in an emergency. The accompanying photo and illustration clearly shows the techniques.

3. FIRE WITH THE BOW AND DRILL

The following bow and drill method is the most common and well-known approach for starting a fire in the wild. The fireboard and spindle must be made of dry and well-seasoned soft wood, such as willow or cottonwood. The fireboard can be as small as two inches by eight inches. Make a small notch for the end of the spindle and a V-shaped groove from the notch to carry the hot, smoldering wood flakes out of the notch. The spindle needs to be at least twelve inches long since it will wear down quickly. The

Striking the spark into the nest of dry grass.

Grasp the flint (or substitute) and steel as shown above. Then strike the edge of the flint. Practice directing the sparks into the starting tinder.

Gently blow on the spark until the flame develops.

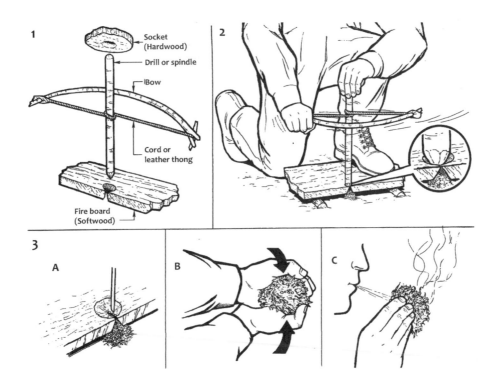

handhold should be made of harder wood. A pine knot works very well. Cut a depression on the handhold to keep the end of the spindle in place. If available, put tallow or other lubricant in the notch to reduce the friction at that end. The bow should be approximately twenty-four inches long and made from stiff, springy wood, such as ash. Notch the ends slightly to keep the string in place. Use a shoelace or other type of cord for the bowstring. A leather thong is best.

Have your starting tinder and twigs ready and at hand. Kneel on the fireboard to hold it in place. Place the end of the spindle into the notch. Wrap the bowstring around the spindle. Place strong, even pressure on the top of the spindle with the handhold. Move the bow back and forth rapidly until glowing sparks appear in the groove. Quickly pick up the fireboard and blow on the embers. As soon as flames appear, add just a little tinder. Then build up until you have enough fire to place in your prepared fire teepee.

4. FIRE WITH THE FIRE SAW

The fire saw method is less well known but requires less complicated construction and material types. Here a softwood log is split, and a V-shaped notch is cut across the log for a "saw" of similar soft wood. A deeper depression is cut down the center, crossing the notch. This can be filled with tinder material, such as lint, dry moss, or pulverized plant fibers. The sawing must be done rapidly back and forth with equal pressure on both ends. Once sparks and embers are produced, use the same procedure as with the bow and drill method.

5. FIRE BY ELECTRICAL SPARK

Any kind of battery-powered device has the potential to create enough heat or a spark sufficient to start a fire. Cell phones, laptops, flashlights, radios, and many other devices can be used to generate heat and sparks. You need to access the positive and negative poles and strike them together intermittently to get a spark. Alternatively, you can short out the two poles with fine wire or steel wool to heat the wire and ignite tinder. Placing a bit of fine steel wool across the poles of a nine-volt battery will demonstrate this method. Of course, any automobile battery will generate a good spark even if it is no longer able to start the vehicle. As always, you need to have paper, dry grass, or other tinder immediately at hand to get a flame going.

6. FIRE BY GUN

If you have a firearm, you have fire. The method of generating a fire using ammunition is described below. But you may need to experiment because every caliber of ammunition and type of gun will act differently. The trick is to blast a bit of burning powder and wadding into a nest of combustibles and gunpowder without blowing them away.

- Remove the bullet from the cartridge.
- Shake most of the powder into a nest of dried grass or other tinder.
- Be sure to place this nest into a depression or crevice to prevent it from being blown away.
- Place some wadding of dry grass or torn cloth into the cartridge on top of the remaining powder.
- Place the cartridge in the firearm and fire it into the nest from about twelve inches away.
- The burning powder flash and wadding should ignite the powdering in the nest.
- Quickly blow the sparks into a full flame and use it to start your fire.

Fire saw.

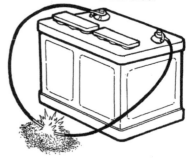

Automotive battery used to start a fire; smaller batteries will work also.

7. FIRE BY SOLAR HEAT

Glasses or a magnifying glass can be used to focus the sun's rays onto tinder to start a fire. The reflector from inside a flashlight can also be used to concentrate sun heat. Much depends on the angle of the sun, the quality and size of the lens, and the temperature and dryness of the tinder. The lens must be held very steady.

8. PREPARING TO START YOUR FIRE

Regardless of how you get that first glowing ember or small flame, building that into a sustainable and effective fire can be challenging. Preparation is the key. You must have all the materials to get you from a small flame to a larger fire assembled and ready before you strike the first match or spark. Start with well-fluffed dry grass, dry rotted wood flakes, pocket lint, or other fibers. Then move to very small twigs or "fuzz sticks." Once burning, these can then be inserted under a small teepee of larger twigs. Finally, larger branches can be added only when a good, hot fire is going. If conditions are wet, place larger branches and logs around the fire to be dried by the heat before using. Building a log reflector behind the fire can reflect fire heat while drying wood for later use.

9. SUSTAINING YOUR FIRE

Dry material with a lot of surface area (fuel) and space in between the area are needed. The bigger the fuel, the larger the area in between needs to be. This is just like fuel-air ratios in an internal-combustion engine. Too much fuel packed together will choke out the fire.

I generally recommend against starting a fire in the rain. The energy use and exposure to water are seldom worth the effort. Seeking shelter and conserving body heat trumps fire building in wet and high-wind conditions. However, once you have a fire going, it can survive a considerable downpour. While small fires are the best, a big fire is necessary to produce a hot enough updraft to vaporize water before it can cool the fuel source. This is why fire hoses often fail to put out building fires. The wet stuff never reaches the red stuff.

When possible, dig a fire pit before starting the fire. This will facilitate better control and retain ashes and hot coals for rekindling, if needed. You can also just fill in the hole to extinguish the fire quickly, if necessary. A deeper pit with a small fire can reduce visibility and focus heat under survival conditions. This is what Rogers' Rangers of the French and Indian Wars did when operating in enemy territory. If you must have a fire overnight, you probably should assign a rotating "fire watch" to keep it going.

10. MAXIMIZING THE HEAT OF YOUR FIRE

Native Americans used to say that "the Indian stays warm by a small fire; the white man stays warm gathering wood." There is some truth to that observation. A small effective fire is usually more efficient than a big one. Big fires draw in cold air. This is why your back gets cold while your front bakes. The vacuum created by the draft passing your body draws the smoke into your face. A small fire with a good reflector on the opposite side and, if possible, a good windbreak/reflector behind you will do much more to keep you warm. I usually carry a large piece of aluminum foil for a reflector and a reflective space blanket or tarp as a lean-to shelter.

If you are going to lie down next to the fire, a long, linear fire and reflector are best. Keep enough fuel within easy reach to add to the fire when you wake up cold. It's no fun getting out of your sleeping bag or shelter to look for wood in the dark. Of course, you want to be far enough from any fire to avoid igniting your clothing, bedding, or shelter. I have seen that happen a few times.

Be sure to clear the area around your fire site of any snow or ice. This turns your site to mud, and you will have a wet camp and wet feet. Be aware of overhead branches and snow-covered limbs as well. You could start a forest fire on one hand or have the melted snow drop down and extinguish your fire, as it did in Jack London's classic "To Build a Fire" short story.

STOVES

There are a variety of commercial and homemade stoves that can be used to more effectively utilize fuel. I have included some of them below.

Various versions of the rocket stove use twigs and small branches in metal stoves to maximize the heat from a little fuel. Using the fuel to heat food and beverages that go into the body is much more efficient than using a campfire, which radiates most of its heat into the air. Shown here (left to right) are a surplus Swiss Army rocket stove, a high-tech stove that generates electricity and has its own fan, and a kettle stove that heats water quickly.

While the homemade hobo stove shown here uses alcohol, it can use twigs or candles as well.

This sand stove is made by filling a can three-quarters full of sand and adding enough gasoline (or other flammable liquid) to soak but not cover the sand. This is a good way to use any available flammable liquid safely and efficiently.

The boiling water bucket (background) is being used to heat up food in cans. The cans are dented, and when the dent pops out, it's time to eat.

Final Thoughts

While fire is not always necessary under survival conditions, it is essential for signaling, boiling water for purification, cooking, and, of course, providing warmth in cold conditions. A fire also offers some primal comfort and security. The ability to start, maintain, and effectively use a fire under difficult circumstances is a fundamental survival skill. On the downside, you can get wet, cold, and exhausted trying to start a fire when you are better off conserving energy and staying dry. You must always use caution to avoid getting burned or starting an uncontrollable fire that will exacerbate your situation.

CHAPTER 12
Ten Shelters You Should Know How to Build

Along with water, food, and medical aid, shelter is one of the prime requirements for survival. In many cases you will need shelter immediately, well before the need for other survival imperatives (e.g., water, food) is evident. Shelter can be found or improvised, and must be appropriate for the hazard. The shelters discussed below should cover the most likely situations.

1. SHELTER AT HOME

Before we talk about shelters on the road and in the woods, let's consider the challenges of maintaining your home as an effective shelter through a disaster. A storm, bomb blast, or civil disorder may damage your roof and blow out your windows. Nearby fires may throw sparks and embers to ignite your home. Looters may attempt to invade your home or set it on fire. Interruption of gas, water, sanitation, and electrical supply may make your home difficult to live in. Assuming that you have plenty of water and food stocked at home, you will need to be prepared to do the following:

- Replace all "normal" services with alternative methods. Have water-gathering and water-filtration methods and tools. Stock plenty of food and medical supplies. Acquire a generator and fuel. Ensure a safe alternative heating system for heating part of your home.
- Replace fire and police services with your own capabilities to extinguish small fires and deter would-be looters and miscreants. You can only hope to deter random small bands of criminals and extinguish small accidental or spark-created fires. General mass disorder or unchecked structural fires in your community will be beyond your capacity to stop. This is why you should be ready and able to evacuate with what you can carry. If these two scenarios are developing, don't wait until it's too late and safe routes are no longer available. Multiple fire extinguishers and adequate firearms may be enough to secure your home against limited threats. The fewer adults or children over the age of fourteen you have, the harder it will be to fight fires and defend against intruders. If you have fewer than four active defenders, you will probably be overwhelmed and should consider evacuation in all cases.

- Repair and reconfigure as needed to prevent damage and provide shelter throughout the crisis. This means having a good supply of heavy-duty plastic sheeting, lumber, nails, tape, and tools. If you have room to store plywood, that would be recommended. You will also need a ladder for reaching the roof. Have a plan and supplies needed to seal off and heat just one or two rooms. If flooding is a danger or you depend on a sump pump for a dry basement, you should have a generator just big enough to maintain the pump or have a plan to clear out and write off the basement. (See Chapter 3, "Ten Items for the Prepared Home.")

2. ABANDONED BUILDINGS

Under survival conditions, normal social and legal restrictions must be abandoned. If you need shelter, any available building is fair game. In such situations, many homes will be unoccupied by their owners because they have fled or could not get back home. Barns, garages, and sheds may also be available. In urban areas there are usually plenty of abandoned houses and commercial buildings. Out in the country and woodlands, you can find plenty of sheds, barns, and vacation cabins. While breaking into someone's home or business is not something we want to do, it may be necessary to get out of the cold, wind, rain, and other hazards. Entry should be achieved with the minimum of noise and damage. A broken window or door will attract unwanted attention. Carrying a lock pick gun or small pry bar in your survival pack may be worth the weight. If you enter someone's home, be respectful of the property. If you must "borrow" food or other items to survive, leave a note for the owners and an IOU for future reimbursement. The breakdown of civilization does not justify your becoming a looter. Most important, be sure it is an unoccupied structure before approaching or attempting entry. Carefully observe, call out, and even knock first. Going from a desperate survivor to an intruder could result in disaster for you and the occupants.

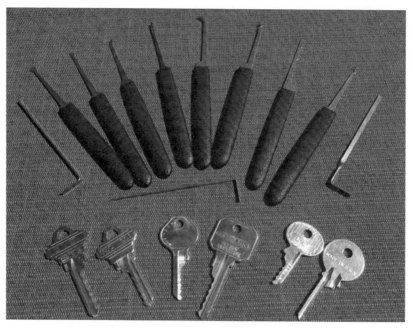

A good set of lock picks and bump keys (shown at right) can add a lot of shelter options in an urban and suburban environment. Learning to use them is not too difficult with frequent practice. (See Chapter 5, "Ten Things you Should Have In your Survival Pack[s].")

Hunting and vacation cabins are found even in wilderness areas. Owners often stock them with supplies and leave them unoccupied for most of the year.

3. FALLOUT SHELTERS

During the Cold War, fallout shelter construction was a major survival topic in the United States. Many of the Civil Defense instructions for building so-called improvised home shelters would have required too much time and exposure to be of much help. Large-scale nuclear events are much less likely today but still not impossible. Localized events are better handled by evacuating the down-wind fallout footprint than by sheltering in place. If you are caught in a radioactive fallout situation and cannot get out, you need to get as much mass between you and the outdoors and stay there as long as possible. In large buildings, get to the lowest

This old Civil Defense illustration shows how an improvised fallout shelter could be quickly built.

levels and most central location. At home, get to the basement and pile dens, solid stuff above and around your shelter area. Staying in the basement under a heavy table or workbench piled with books, metal, wood, or other materials will significantly reduce your exposure. Radioactivity declines by a factor of ten for every sevenfold increase in time, so the longer you can stay in shelter, the less your total exposure level will be. Of course, being able to stay in the shelter depends on your having food, water, sanitation, and other supplies in place. The old Civil Defense recommended shelter time was two weeks. If you are exposed to fallout, you need to get out of the exposed clothing and decontaminate yourself before entering the shelter. Advanced shelter construction and decontamination are too complex to cover here. Below are some basic shelter illustrations.

4. TENTS

Obviously, tents are effective shelters. Many modern camping tents are huge, heavy, multi-room facilities that are not easily transported or heated. The challenge is to have the right tent for your needs. If you are going to have to carry it, then weight and compactness are the first priorities. The tent you choose should be roomy enough for you (and your party) and your gear. You do not want to be up against the damp, cold tent wall or be forced to leave your equipment outside. Flat-walled tents are unnecessarily bulky and vulnerable to wind. Modern dome tents are light, strong, and quick to put up. Remember that you can put up your tent inside your house if the heat goes off. A tent is far easier to heat and light than a room or house.

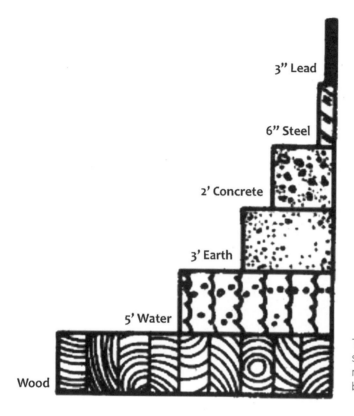

This illustration shows the comparative shielding of various materials. The heavier the material, the better the protection, but even books and furniture help.

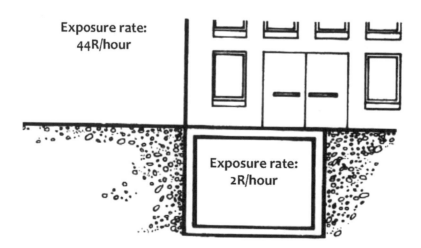

The above illustration shows the great reduction in radiation exposure achieved by simply getting below ground. The center of the basement would be even better.

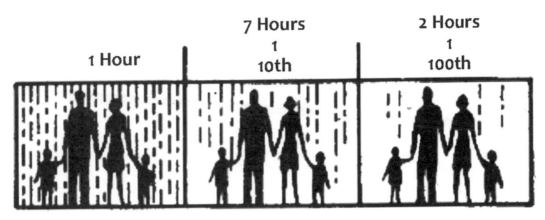

The above illustrates how radiation decays over time by a factor of ten for every sevenfold factor of time. The general recommendation is to remain in as much shelter as possible for as many hours as possible for at least two weeks. This was for a massive nuclear exchange. Limited nuclear strikes or incidents would create less initial radiation and thus shorter shelter times.

This winter tent is ideal for cold-weather use. Its small size retains more heat and offers less wind resistance. Note the porch that can be used for gear storage.

5. TARPS AND PONCHOS

The lowly tarpaulin is an oft-overlooked necessity of disaster survival and recovery. These sheets of material can protect you, your equipment, and your supplies from rain, sun, wind, cold, and even some airborne contaminants. Having the right kind and size of tarpaulin in the right place will be critical in many aspects of survival and property protection. A tarpaulin also can be used as a rainfly over a tent or as a ground cloth under one.

Field Shelter

A tarp is just a tent without a shape. Carrying a large enough sheet of plastic or other waterproof material can provide you with a wide variety of shelter options. It can also be used to gather water, cover a solar water still, or make an improvised rain poncho. A space blanket is just a small reflective tarp. If weight and space are issues, you can easily fit a 10 to 20-foot by one-mil thick plastic painter's tarp into any survival pack to provide short-term protection. I usually carry a space blanket and some kind of tarp in all my survival packs and kits. I can set up a variety of shelter configurations, depending on conditions. The tarp can also just be thrown over me as a hasty shelter, if necessary. I keep a heavier 20x25-foot nylon tarp in my vehicle. I use it to cover the entire vehicle when camping.

Home Survival

Tarps are an absolute necessity on any home survival supply list. Even lightweight plastic painter's tarps can be effective in closing off a single room to preserve heat or to reduce infiltration of hazardous dusts and mists. They are easy and fast to put up with masking tape or duct tape. Heavier polyethylene tarps can be used to cover broken windows or damaged roofs. Make sure that the tarps are over the roof peek or tucked under the shingles at the high end to keep water from running underneath. In a worst-case scenario, they can be used to make a shelter away from the house if it's no longer safe.

Using A Stone As A Grommet

Most tarps come with grommets for tying them down, but some (like the cheap plastic ones) do not. Also, you may want to shape the tarp into a tent or shelter with ties in the center. There are several commercially made devices for this, but you can simply take a rounded stone, wrap the tarp material around it, and tie a line around the bulge.

Clear Plastic Painter's Tarps

Thin plastic painters tarps are cheap and lightweight. A 9x12-foot by one-mil thick tarp costs about two dollars. These are great for sealing indoor rooms and for fast one-time shelters. They do not hold up well in strong winds, but they are just as waterproof as any tent. One of these should be in every survival pack. I recommend the 12x20 size. I have built hasty dome-like shelters out of three-mil plastic in the winter that kept out cold winds and snow. They also had the added benefit of greenhouse-like solar heating on sunny days. I built one of heavier plastic in a Wisconsin winter, and it was at least twenty degrees warmer inside. I left it up for a year and used it again the next fall.

Opaque Plastic With Grommets

These are the tarps designed for covering things outdoors. They are heavier and come with grommets on the edges. They can be formed into all kinds of shelters. You can get them in camouflage, green, and brown, and with reflective material on one side. An 8x10-foot brown/reflective tarp costs about eight dollars, and a 12x 16-foot model costs about sixteen dollars. Used as a lean-to shelter in front of a campfire, the reflective tarps can greatly increase warmth. They are also effective as an outer covering for tents in winter.

Canvas Tarps

These are rather heavy and expensive but are more durable and will resist wind much better. They generally come in white (for winter], green, and gray. They are far too heavy for a backpack but are good for home and vehicle packs. An 8x10 canvas tarp will cost about forty dollars. They make the best for shelters if you don't have to carry them far.

Examples of tarps rigged for shelter.

Top: Cheap 3-mil 12x20-foot poly drop cloth on top of heavy canvas painter's tarp. Below: Black and aluminized (heat reflection or absorption) polyethylene tarp next to another version of polyethylene tarp.

Typical canvas tarp shelter. Note the fire reflector branches in front.

6. DEBRIS HUTS

The debris hut is the classic "survival shelter" made from branches, grass, and foliage. Building a truly waterproof debris hut takes considerable time and energy. They offer effective wind protection and significant heat containment. A well-built debris hut can fend off a light rain for a while but will usually leak in a prolonged or heavy downpour. The steeper the angle and the more overlapping layers you have, the better the rain protection you will get.

This teepee/debris shelter is strong, but you need to find or cut a good number of long poles and they will leak at the top center. Of course, you can put a small fire (note the smoke) in the center for providing warmth and repelling insects, and the updraft tends to deflect light rain.

Two examples of debris huts in Alaska.

Tripod shelters are strong and fast to put up. They are better at conserving body heat but do not reflect and gather heat from a campfire very well.

Typical lean-to shelter made from natural materials.

The dome shelter above is strong and can be built with or without an open side, depending on whether you will have a fire or will be conserving heat inside. All you need to do is find bendable saplings. You can cover it with natural or man-made materials. One of these that I built lasted more than two years.

7. NATURAL SHELTERS

Animals generally do not build shelters; they just use what nature provides. Large pine trees, rock overhangs, caves, large uprooted trees, and thick shrub foliage all offer some wind and rain protection. Natural shelter offers fast protection with minimum energy expenditure. Even if you have a tarp or other shelter material, using it to enhance an already sheltered place will be more effective.

A fallen tree becomes the start of a sturdy shelter.

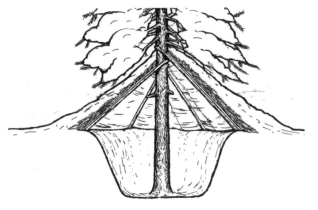

The natural shelter of this pine tree is enhanced by a layer of pine boughs and snow to create a good shelter.

This poncho shelter uses heavy foliage to enhance its wind protection and camouflage.

8. SNOW SHELTERS

A snow shelter may be your only option in some cases. I have built some nice igloo-type shelters by using large snowballs, as you would ice blocks. The inside temperature stayed at about 32 degrees even when it was much colder outside. The problem was that I got wet and used a lot of energy building them. When finding or building other shelters and starting a fire are impossible, digging a snow-trench shelter or making a cave into a drift may be your only option.

9. BEST AVAILABLE SHELTER IN AN EMERGENCY

In some cases the need for shelter is immediate and absolute. These situations include during earthquakes, tornadoes, and terrorist attacks. In such cases, you have to use the *best available* shelter rather than risk running to the *best* shelter.

   Earthquakes strike without warning. A slight rattle may escalate to a building-collapsing event within seconds. Running into the street or standing in a doorway is not an effective defense. Getting under a bed, desk, or other furniture is also not advisable. If the building collapses, the furniture will collapse and then crush you. Even a car will be crushed flat and the tires flattened under debris. The safest location is right at the base of a wall or next to your car, desk, or similar strong object. Yes, these will be crushed somewhat, but not flattened. The debris will stop and be held up a few feet on either side of the crushed object, leaving a gap. This is known as the "triangle of life," where most survivors are found.

   Tornadoes develop and move quickly. Unlike earthquakes, tornadoes lift and throw debris, so getting under any kind of heavy shelter offers protection. In any building, move toward the inner and lower parts of the building. In commercial structures, the interior fire escape stairwells are usually reinforced. If you are in your vehicle,

into a drift it may be your only option.

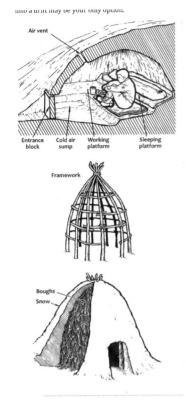

Top: Building this snow cave shelter would be much better than remaining exposed outside. Note the cold air sump and sleeping shelf. Cold air sinks, so a shelf a few feet above the floor could be five to ten degrees warmer.

Center and bottom: Bent saplings formed into a dome and covered first with boughs and then with snow. This is much safer and requires less effort than building a pure snow shelter.

do not try to outrun the tornado! If you can drive at a 90-degree angle out of the storm's path, do so. But if that is not possible, pull over and evacuate our vehicle. Seek shelter in the nearest solid building or storm shelter. If nothing is available, lie down in a low place or ditch. Cover your head with your arms. Never get under a vehicle, as it may roll over and crush you. Underpasses are not good shelters since they actually accelerate the winds and can suck vehicles and people out.

Suicide bombers, armed terrorists, and gang shooters can emerge at any location where people work, play, study, worship, or gather. If you are observant, you may be lucky enough to note suspicious persons with packages or bulging clothing, but you may not know that you are in danger until the first shots or explosions occur. Quite often there will be more than one shooter or more than one bomb. You need to hit the floor immediately without hesitation. Unless you know exactly where the shooters/bombers are, stay down and do not move. If you can see that the assailants are not looking at you or are reloading, and an exit or substantial "cover" is close by, crawl to that. Get as much solid mass between you and the threat as possible. Concealment behind a table or plasterboard wall is better than nothing but will not stop bullets or blast fragments. If possible, seek cover behind masonry walls, vehicles, or heavy appliances, or in low places. Once the immediate attack has subsided, leave the area because there is often a secondary or delayed attack as well. (See Chapter 6, "Ten Ways to Avoid and Survive Street Crime.")

10. VEHICLE AS SHELTER

The automobile is the most ubiquitous and available shelter to be found in most parts of the populated world. In many scenarios, you would already be in a motor vehicle when the survival emergency begins. Automobiles are waterproof, windproof, and usually fairly comfortable, but they are poorly insulated metal and glass boxes that radiate away your heat in cold weather and become solar ovens in hot weather. Still, they will provide better and faster wind, rain, and snow protection than most improvised shelters you could build, so unless you have the alternative of a shelter and fire combination or a good tent, a vehicle is a good shelter.

You can use your survival kit items (e.g., space blanket, wool blanket) to improve warmth, and a few candles will raise the temperature significantly. The location of the vehicle is also critical. If you want to be rescued, stay on main roads and with the vehicle, but if things have gone very bad, you want to get off (and out of sight from) any main road. Camouflage the auto with snow, foliage, or other covering. Under civil disorder conditions, don't even consider staying in your vehicle on a main road or urban/suburban street. You are in a big flammable tin target. In hot weather, use the vehicle only for shade and to anchor your shade canopy.

If you are trapped in your vehicle in a storm or cold conditions, run the motor every hour for about ten minutes to keep the battery charged and the vehicle a bit warm. Be sure that the tailpipe is kept clear of snow and the window is slightly open to prevent carbon monoxide poisoning. Place a bright colored flag outside the vehicle to attract help. Unless you can see better shelter or rescue close by, stay in the vehicle until help arrives or conditions improve. You should always have the following items in your vehicle:

- Sleeping bag or wool blanket or, at the minimum, an aluminized plastic survival blanket
- Candles (tea candles are best), matches, and aluminum foil to help warm vehicle
- Emergency food items, such as energy bars or Lifeboat Rations
- Water (at least one or two quarts)
- A good flashlight (check batteries regularly)
- Road flares and reflectors
- Jumper cables
- Towing chain or rope
- Small shovel
- Cat litter or old carpet sections (12x36 feet) to get vehicle out of snow and ice
- A first aid kit
- A small, portable survival kit to carry with you if you need to abandon your vehicle (see Chapter 4, "Ten Items You Should Always Carry," and Chapter 5, "Ten Items You Should Have in Your Survival Pack(s)"). Reduce the size and quantity of items to fit in your vehicle pack.

CHAPTER 13
Terrorism

Terrorism is a symptom of our larger "perfect storm" disintegration of economic stability and national integrity. Practiced by extremists, criminals, and rogue nations, it will increase in frequency and variety throughout the coming decades.

First, I must point out that this chapter does not contain "ten principles," as have the previous chapters, but it is required reading for concerned citizens who are making preparations for self-reliance during an emergency.

Terrorism is not in and of itself an "ism." Terror is a tactic or method employed by an "ism" to further a political, religious, or economic agenda. Because terror by definition creates panic and confusion, these acts generate false information and confused reports. In addition, these events can be twisted, misrepresented, and exploited by the government and special interests to further various agendas. For this reason, it is difficult to determine the truth about these kinds of events. It is best to focus on avoiding them, surviving them, and dealing with their aftermath. The "who" and "why" are irrelevant. Regardless of the sources or motivations of the terrorists, the results are the same for the citizens: immediate injury or death, social and economic damage, and intensified security and regulation of life. Terror generates fear and confusion, and this leads to acceptance of tyranny. Security at any price is the choice of many irresponsible and misled citizens. Public involvement, vigilance, and responsibility are the choices of survivors and free people.

Terror tactics (e.g., bombings, shootings) are the only options left to extremists and Third World government agents faced with the new technology of satellites, drones, smart weapons, and surveillance systems. These factions cannot wage any kind of conventional warfare or guerrilla operations without being quickly exterminated. Terror, sabotage, and resistance tactics are effective, cheap, and difficult to prevent. Since terror cells or individuals require little or no coordination or chain of command, they are impossible to roll up or disrupt. All they need are an extremist philosophy and how-to information. Regrettably, hate groups and radical religious leaders are able to use the Internet to promote hate and violence while providing the technical information on how to implement these actions.

SOURCES OF TERRORIST MOTIVATION AND SUPPORT

Terrorists are motivated by a negative view of some part of the population. They may believe that their acts will disable their "enemies," or they may simply be satisfied with revenge for some wrong, perceived or actual. Their reasoning may be founded on imaginary ideas, or it may be rooted in actual injustice and harm done by others. Innocent civilians who have little to do with the issue always wind up as targets. Lone individuals may generate acts of terror without any outside support, or they may get training, targeting, and supply support from an organization or a foreign government.

Domestic

Unfortunately, there are some individuals and groups in America who feel that acts of violence and destruction can make a statement or in some way further their cause. These motivations include environmental protection, racial hatred, religious fanaticism, economic injustice, and political frustration. Unfortunately, a lot of the media misrepresents these extremists as being representative of "survivalists" or "patriots." Terrorism is not an element of any true survivalist or patriotic philosophy or organization.

Foreign Governments

Foreign governments can critically damage America's economy, infrastructure, and stability without any form of overt act of war or invasion. Modern high-density populations and high-tech infrastructures are so interconnected and dependent that even small, well-targeted attacks can have huge impacts. The 9/11 attacks were actually fairly small but have cost our economy hundreds of billions of dollars on security that could have been spent to reduce the debt or repair our aging infrastructure. Iran, China, and many other nations can cripple our computerized banking, water, power, and transportation systems with untraceable viruses.

Special Interests

While I do not want to subscribe to conspiracy theories, it is not too far-fetched to imagine that those wanting to expand government powers or make money on security services or devices might directly or indirectly facilitate some form of terrorism, when you consider the billions of dollars taken and the expansion of powers resulting from each event. Since you can do little, if anything, about such operations, your most effective action is to reduce their effects and spread preparedness.

Foreign Nongovernment Entities

Probably the two most active nongovernment foreign terror sources are radical Islamic organizations and drug cartels. For the reasons stated above, the religious extremists have resorted to motivating and training multiple terrorists and dispersing them without further management or a chain of command. This results in hundreds of terrorists and sleepers acting individually or in small teams while the leaders and motivators hide behind religious and speech protections. The drug cartels of South America and Europe currently confine their methods to intimidation and shootings within communities, but they use street gangs and gang members as surrogate soldiers. In other countries where the citizens are unarmed and the police are already controlled and intimidated, the extremists have no qualms about using bombs and mass executions.

CIVILIANS ARE THE TARGETS

Anarchists often target government offices and officials. Misguided persons often react to a perceived government injustice, such as what happened in Oklahoma City or at various abortion clinics. Many also focus their attacks on these targets, but these acts still result in the "collateral damage" deaths of civilians. In the vast majority of terrorist attacks, the targets are civilians.

Terror is generated most effectively by a high body count. Disabling a nation or a society is dependent on killing and paralyzing its population. Remember that major cities were (and still are) the targets of Cold War nuclear missiles. During World War II, the Allies could not bomb factories out of action, so they switched to bombing the civilian residential areas to kill and disable the workers and their families. Virtually every terrorist act has been directed at killing and maiming a high number of civilian men, women, and children, yet all of the funding, equipment, and training for so-called homeland security has been directed to noncivilian agencies and programs. A cold shoulder has been given to private efforts to educate and activate civilians for their own defense. Switzerland and Israel have set examples for mass involvement of the people to prevent terrorism and foreign attacks. So while civilians are the front-line targets and most probable victims of terrorist attacks in America, they are left with little training or equipment to cope with the variety of threats they will face. It is left to responsible preparedness and self-reliance organizations to activate and educate the public for their own immediate and long-term defense and independence.

TERRORIST METHODS AND WEAPONS

Bombs and Arson

Conventional explosive devices and improvised explosive devices (IEDs) are easy to make. Various terrorist manuals and websites provide details on bomb-making and detonation systems. Ammonium nitrate fertilizer, LP gas cylinders, and common "gunpowder" are just a few options available to would-be terrorists. Military-grade high explosives—such as TNT, amatol, PETN, C-4, and C-12—are harder to get but can be smuggled into the United States or stolen from military sites. Bombs can be used to create mass casualties or destroy key infrastructure. They can be enhanced by the addition of flammables or shrapnel. While the so-called fuel-air technique of using a small explosive to distribute fuel vapor or dust that is then ignited by a second explosion has not been used by terrorists yet, such devices can reach near nuclear devastation levels. We can anticipate a continued escalation of bomb use against public assemblies.

Arson is probably the cheapest method of mass destruction available. The so-called hell nights in Detroit provide evidence of the terror this method can bring. One or two individuals with a small amount of accelerant can set dozens of fires. A truly planned campaign of strategically placed fires could easily overwhelm fire departments and lay waste to whole communities.

Mass Shootings and Snipers

If a person is determined to shoot up a shopping mall or a public gathering, no amount of regulations or security can prevent it. Armed citizens can limit such events by quickly putting down the shooter, but some casualties will result. This method is far more common in disarmed Middle Eastern and European nations than in the United States. Random shootings can have a great terror effect, literally paralyzing a community.

Targeted assassinations can have significant (if unpredictable) political impacts. This method of terror was certainly predominant in the 1960s but has been less frequent since. Sniper weapons and technology have advanced greatly since then, and we can only anticipate how extremists may use sniping again. Snipers require considerable training, an easy-to-conceal (disassembled) weapon, and usually a partner/spotter. We can expect foreign or group involvement at some level when this method is employed.

Biological weapons

Probably the most feared terrorist weapons involve biological agents. Biological weapons are cheap and easy to manufacture, difficult to detect, and easy to disperse. Bacterial agents (e.g., anthrax, plague, typhus) and viruses (e.g., smallpox, influenza, and encephalitis) are just some of the agents available. These agents can be sprayed into a public place, such as a train station or concert hall, where the unknowing victims will carry the diseases back to their homes and communities. By the time the first symptoms appear in emergency rooms and doctors' offices, millions of people will have been infected and the numbers will keep multiplying.

Once employed, these agents regenerate and spread themselves. After an epidemic is started, the police and fire departments are overwhelmed. The people who run the hospitals, water supplies, garbage pickup, food deliveries, and other vital services are sick or stay home to avoid contamination. The whole economy and infrastructure collapse. Civil disorder, fires, shortages, and panic will result in even more deaths. There is no doubt that this kind of attack (or natural event) will likely occur in the next few decades. Even a handful of sprinkled flour in a mass crowd accompanied by a cry of "anthrax!" could kill hundreds in a stampede.

Chemical Weapons and Dirty Bombs

Chemical agents—such as sarin, tabun, and VX—are extremely lethal but relatively difficult for terrorists to manufacture. However, it has been done in a few cases. These nerve agents have a limited area of effect and are usually used in enclosed areas with high concentrations of people, such as the Tokyo subway station sarin attack in 1995. Carrying a bulky chemical mask is impractical, but some charcoal-impregnated folding N-95 masks offer short-term protection, especially if combined with eye protection and a rain poncho of any type.

Dirty bombs are just conventional explosives that disperse some form of radioactive dust around the blast area. The fear of radiation is the primary terror element. If you escape the blast and fragmention, you must avoid breathing the dust and get the dust off you immediately. Get upwind of the dust cloud, strip off your clothing, and wash down any way you can. That N-95 folding mask in your pocket (in plastic bag) just saved your life.

Infrastructure Attacks and Sabotage

During the Cold War many nations planned to resist Soviet occupation through a campaign of sabotage. The Swiss resistance manual titled *Total Resistance* by Major H. Von Dach outlined all sorts of ways to disable railroads, highways, motor vehicles, and electrical systems, and many of these techniques were devilishly easy. Today's systems are even more vulnerable to easy sabotage. I will not detail any of them here, but individuals can knock out power, wreck a train, or blow up a vehicle with common household and pocket materials. Consider the impact of just a random poisoning of crops. We would have to dump the whole harvest. What about those millions of miles of railroad tracks, power lines, pipelines, gas lines, water systems, refineries, and farm fields? No one can protect them all. It is important to keep in mind that there are plenty of explosives and chemical weapons available in our towns, on our highways, and on our railroads that are already there for the terrorists to simply detonate.

DEFENDING AGAINST TERROR

All the survival/preparedness techniques and items so energetically advocated here apply to surviving a terror attack. The ability to remain at home for extended periods is critical in many scenarios. The capacity to evacuate with enough (bug-out bag) items to get to safety without depending on others also will be important in some cases. If you live in a high-density, central urban area, your vulnerability is high even at home. For most people, the dangers are from events while away from home, such as at a workplace, on the road, or in public places. Your only two defenses are situational awareness and pocket preparedness.

Situational Awareness

You cannot simply ignore the possibility of an attack. You must "what if" every situation and raise your threat level of readiness as needed. You have to consider worst-case situations and have a mental plan to avoid or escape any developing situation.

- Never be in the center or front of a crowd where you cannot move or get to an exit, making you vulnerable to being trapped or trampled. Always have an exit plan or two in mind. Stay aware of exit routes. Don't hesitate to cut through back rooms to get out.
- Be aware of people. Does any individual or group of people look suspicious? Is anyone carrying odd packages? Is someone dressed in a way that may conceal large weapons or vest bombs? If something doesn't seem right, it probably isn't!
- Be aware of hazards: unattended packages of any kind, suspicious mists or smoke, the presence of potential explosives or chemical poisons (e.g., pool chemicals, LP gas cylinders, fertilizer, gasoline) that could be detonated by terrorists.
- Be aware of targets. Are you in a large crowd or a busy public place (e.g., sporting event, celebration, shopping mall, rail station) that may be targeted? Stay alert anytime you are in or near high-hazard industrial site, such as chemical plants or public buildings.
- As a good citizen, If you see something suspicious or hazardous, say something to available security or by calling 911.

Pocket Preparedness

The survival adage that "it's not what you have; it's what you have with you" applies doubly for terrorist events. Here are some items you should always have with you:

- An N-95 folding dust/mist pocket mask should be tucked into every coat, jacket, and bag. These can provide immediate protection against biological agents and toxic dust. They are also helpful against chemicals and smoke long enough for you to escape.
- A small LED flashlight lets you see when the lights go out or the place fills with dust and smoke to find your way out and be spotted by rescuers.
- Bandanas are handy for "help" flags, emergency bandages and tourniquets, and improvised face masks.
- A good whistle can be used to summon help or direct panicked people.

Although some places prohibit the carrying of knives and firearms, I cannot overemphasize their importance wherever possible. Desperate times require desperate measures.

Conclusions

As social, economic, and political conditions worsen over the next decades, terrorist acts of various kinds will increase. The nature of these attacks and their targets are limited only by the terrorists' imagination. The unthinkable is exactly what they think of and make happen. Terrorist acts seldom achieve any political or social objective. Often, the result of such acts is the opposite of what was perceived in the troubled minds of the terrorists. The immediate effects of any terrorist act are death, injury, and destruction visited on innocent citizens. The best a citizen can do is be alert, avoid potential targets, and be prepared to survive the injuries and disruptions created. The greater effects of terrorist acts are political panic and state paranoia, which lead to greater and greater surveillance, monitoring, regulation, prohibitions, and even confiscations in the name of security. This indirect effect is the most terrifying of all. Life without freedom is not worth the price of security. Life without freedom is not life at all.

ABOUT THE AUTHOR

James. C. Jones was born on the Southside of Chicago at the beginning of World War II. An impoverished and chaotic childhood made him a natural survivalist from a very early age. He put together his own survival pack at age twelve and often spent time in the woodlands and swamps that adjoined the city at that time. Working two jobs while living in one room and attending high school in the tough Southside added more real-world survival experiences. He started as a technician at a large chemical manufacturing complex, where his passion for safety led him to become an award-winning safety manager. While acquiring certifications in emergency medicine, hazardous chemical handling, safety management, and training management related to his job, he energetically pursued survival-related outdoor activities, including rock climbing, caving, rafting, horseback riding, and survival camping.

Jones founded Live Free USA in the late 1960s and helped it evolve from an outdoor survival club into a broad-based national preparedness and self-reliance education organization. During the 1970s and 1980s, he was a leading voice in defending and defining responsible survivalism on national television and radio programs and to the international media. While interest in self-reliance waned somewhat in the 1990s, he worked to hold the movement together and sustain the networks that still existed. When the events and trends of the twenty-first century rekindled interest and support for survival education and self-reliance, he became active in the newly titled "prepper" movement.

The author returning from a week-long survival hike in the 1960s.

Jones has developed and conducted hundreds of survival training events and seminars over the past forty years and has written hundreds of articles for Live Free's newsletter, *American Survivor*. He is now retired and living in Indiana and currently writes articles for several national preparedness and survival-related publications, while continuing to teach a variety of survival courses and make presentations at major preparedness expositions.